The Little Book
The Ungodly Liberal Agenda

by

Charles Edwards

authorHOUSE®

AuthorHouse™
1663 Liberty Drive
Bloomington, IN 47403
www.authorhouse.com
Phone: 1-800-839-8640

© 2010 Charles Edwards. All rights reserved.

No part of this book may be reproduced, stored in a retrieval system, or transmitted by any means without the written permission of the author.

First published by AuthorHouse 3/10/2010

ISBN: 978-1-4490-7229-2 (e)
ISBN: 978-1-4490-7228-5 (sc)

Library of Congress Control Number: 2010900452
Printed in the United States of America
Bloomington, Indiana

This book is printed on acid-free paper.

Contents

PROLOGUE		ix
1.	SWEET 'N SOUR Sweet in the Mouth – Bitter in the Belly	1
	Political dieting	2
	Depraved definition	4
	Freedom to fall short	5
	A two-party nightmare	6
2.	ATHEISM A Suggestion to Mankind that there is no God	9
	False Accusations	10
	Twisting the Truth	13
	A Contagious Disease	15
	Equal rights	16
	Intolerance	17
	Hatred	18
	The Christians Will Rule	19
3.	FEMINISM Takes away the Masculine Authority of God	23
	God	23
	Jesus	25
	Husbands and Wives	27
	Family	28
	Homosexuality	30

4.	**ANIMAL RIGHTS** Removes the Fact of being Created in God's Image	33
	Image of God	34
	Different Flesh	35
	The Outcome	38
5.	**ENVIRONMENTALISM** Exchanges Worship of God for Worship of the Earth.	41
	The Creator	43
	Perversion	44
	Creation Suffers	47
	Knowledge	50
	Provision	53
	Judgment	54
	The Outcome	57
6.	**EDUCATION** The Liberal Pollution of the Minds of Children	59
	Church and State	60
	School Prayer	63
	Secularism	65
	Curriculum	69
	Money	72
	Solution	74
7.	**GOVERNMENT** Encourages Trust in Human Institutions	77
	Trust	77
	Purpose	81

	Deceit	85
	Taxes	90
	Suppression	94
	Remedy	98
8.	**ABORTION** Deceives Mankind into Self-annihilation	103
	Life	105
	Foreknowledge	109
	Selection	110
	Sacrifice	113
	Penalties	114
EPILOGUE		117

PROLOGUE

I HAVE WRITTEN this book to the Christian believer, intending to provide information on the great war between God and Satan in the struggle for the souls of mankind. It was not written to prove the existence of God, the truth of the Bible, or the deity of Christ. I choose to use my time and talent to help the believer have a better understanding of God's eternal purpose rather than wasting my time arguing such things with an unbeliever.

All of the major issues of the day concerning race, religion, culture, and morality are being used by Satan as methods of enticing people away from God. All of these issues are found in the ungodly liberal philosophy and can be identified as such by comparing them to scripture.

While it is true that the Bible does not use the names of today when speaking of countries, individuals, or practices, God has layered different meanings upon most Bible verses that can apply to different people in different times. Many of the prophetic verses that applied to Israel's (and other countries') Old Testament future also have meaning for our time and the end time yet to come. Otherwise, it would not be a book for the ages.

If the contents of the Bible only had meaning for the Biblical age, then, after understanding that we are saved from sin through Jesus Christ, the rest of the Bible would be irrelevant to us. Godly people should not allow the ungodly to lead them into such a false belief.

Charles Edwards

In II Peter 1:20, 21 we read, *But know this first of all, that no prophecy of Scripture is a matter of one's own interpretation, for no prophecy was ever made by an act of human will, but men moved by the Holy Spirit spoke from God.*

What these verses tell us is that since all Biblical prophecy was inspired by God through the Holy Spirit, it can only be interpreted the same way – through instruction by the Spirit. The Bible is a spiritual book written for spiritual people. If one has not been born of the Spirit, that one will never have a spiritual understanding of God's word. To be born of the Spirit means to personally receive the Holy Spirit as an indwelling entity, giving the believer (receiver) a new spiritual nature, without which, there is no true communion with God.

A further understanding of the Holy Spirit's teaching nature can be found by reading John 16:7-15. It can't be said that this passage was for the apostles only, because verse 8 says, *"and He, when He comes, will convict the world concerning sin, and righteousness, and judgment."* The Holy Spirit's influence reaches through all believers to the end of the age.

It also says in verse 13, *"But when He, the Spirit of truth, comes, He will guide you into all the truth; for He will not speak on His own initiative, but whatever He hears, He will speak; and He will disclose to you what is to come."* God will instruct the Spirit to reveal to us a particular meaning from a particular verse at a particular time.

As Moses was restating the law in Deuteronomy, he posed the question in 18:21, *"And you may say in your heart, 'How shall we know the word which the Lord has not spoken?'"* Good question. If any interpretation does not conform to the overall theme of the Bible, then it is not from God. Therein lies the extreme importance of studying the entire Bible to understand the complete message.

Moses said to the people in Deut. 29:29, *The secret things belong to the Lord our God, but the things revealed belong to us and to our sons forever, that we may observe all the words of this law.* That applies to the New Covenant as well as the Old.

When God spoke to the people of the Old Testament, for example, concerning morality, the same word applies to all people of all ages since God changes not. Our social customs may change but God's laws of morality do not change. If Israel or any people of that time was condemned for immorality, the same condemnation can extend to America in the twenty-first century. And, the same can be said for promises of blessing.

Unless otherwise noted, all of the Bible references in this book are taken from the New American Standard Translation published in 1978. It is an updated work of the American Standard Version published in 1901.

Charles Edwards

Chapter One

SWEET 'N SOUR

Sweet in the Mouth – Bitter in the Belly

In the book of Revelation, chapter 10, the apostle John recorded a strange story. While receiving a vision of things to come in the latter days, a magnificent angel appeared, having an open, little book in his hands. The angel cried out, causing other angelic voices to do the same, but when John started to write what he heard (as he had been doing throughout the vision) another voice told him to seal up the things that had been spoken and *"do not write them."*

Then, an even stranger thing happened. The "voice from heaven" told John to go and take the little book from the hand of the angel, who said to John, *"take it, and eat it; and it will make your stomach bitter, but in your mouth it will be sweet as honey."* (Rev. 10:9) After eating the book, John found that it did taste good in the mouth, sweet as honey, but after swallowing, his stomach became very bitter.

If any story from the Bible can be used to describe cause and effect in the lives of people, whether as a group or as individuals, this one can. How often have we all eaten the "little book" as we worked our way through this life? We take a bite of some pleasurable idea, enjoying the sweetness and the good feeling that we're sure will continue, bringing happiness and fulfillment. But after swallowing the great idea, comes the bitter pangs of regret as we realize how overrated the promise was, how we considered the plan with too-narrow vision, and how we based the decision on emotion and desire rather than fact and need.

The worst thing about it is that it happens with great frequency to individuals and nations in spite of the history of our lives and that of the world. How many times do some folks suffer the bellyache of financial setbacks, sometimes ruin, after enjoying the sweet taste of unlimited spending? Or the pain of shattered relationships after the sweet talk of disguised self interests?

Whole groups of people will joyfully bite into the pleasant tasting rhetoric of some would-be dictator, anarchist, or politician running for office, whose ideology appears to be the magic elixir for all ills, at least the ones that are currently getting the most press. But once that great pretender slips into the belly of the system and begins weaving his deceit throughout the body, much pain develops among the populace in the form of confiscatory taxes, limited freedom, shortage of necessities, and, in extreme cases, persecution, imprisonment and death.

An example still in the memory of senior citizens is that of the German people who swallowed Hitler's big lie during the 1930s of the sweet promise of being number one in the world, but in the 1940s vomited up the truth of their sickness in the form of racism and genocide for all the world to see. And, in the period when the Nazis came to power, Germany was the most educated country in the world. So much for education without wisdom and understanding.

Political dieting

Our country today has many people who are telling us that, pertaining to political ideology, we are eating wrong, and if we will only swallow their sweet, medicinal words, all ills will be conquered. Beware of the pain in the belly. Such persons are politicians in Washington D.C. and state capitols, professors in college, editors in newsrooms, TV newsmen and reporters, Hollywood stars, and many activist organizations.

These people are of the liberal persuasion who are more than willing to shoulder our burdens if we only give them the power and control required for them to bring about total peace and harmony across the land, (and eventually the world) where every need is met. They all are working on their own little item of the overall agenda, and may not realize any collusion, but they are all working toward the same end – the unlearned many controlled by the elite few.

The language of the liberals appeals to our emotions in an attempt to get us to accept any law, regulation, or court ruling that supposedly enhances the lives of the have-nots. Such changes are portrayed as necessary to eliminate hunger, disease, poverty, homelessness, and any other thing the "deprived" are doing without. All of these conditions are prevalent in most third-world countries, but we're told that the same is true here in the United States, the richest country in the world.

What are we to make of it when a prominent, national politician tells us that thirty million people in this country are going to bed hungry? Thirty million? In a country with a population of three hundred million? That's ten percent of our population! With all of the government welfare programs and entitlements, the shelters and charities, the trillions of dollars spent on the war on poverty since the sixties, we still have one out of every ten people going to bed hungry?

That's what we are told, but we're not told where such figures come from or what caused those unfortunate people to be mired in those circumstances. Those are questions we're not supposed to ask. All that's expected of us is to willingly give more of our hard-earned money in taxes and allow the politicians and government regulators to be in full control of our resources.

Another favorite liberal tactic is to encourage us to "do it for the children," a twist on our emotions if ever there was one. How could anyone not do something for the children? That is, of course, the children who have been allowed to be born.

Depraved definition

The liberal philosophy is based on depraved human nature, the condition of men since the garden of Eden and appeals to greed and selfishness while attributing such characteristics to the conservatives. They tell their constituents they deserve more and they shouldn't be expected to exert any uncomfortable effort in acquiring the material of their need.

Some folks of the liberal persuasion don't like to hear their views described as ungodly or as something "wrong," citing a more palatable definition as one who is generous, tolerant, and favoring reform. Those are wonderful words that supposedly describe the well-meaning efforts of our liberal caretakers but in reality are the words of ravenous wolves in sheep's clothing, (mentioned by Jesus in Matt. 7:15) spoken to tickle the ears of all those who are ruled by the aforementioned depraved human nature.

That word "progress" is often used to bring about change that results in more harm than good, and while we are bombarded with numbers that show why such action is needed, we are never given the numbers showing how many were helped and how many were hurt as a result of a particular debacle. The do-gooders are never called to answer for their errors in miscalculation, much in the same way the spiritualists who make their yearly predictions in January are never called for explanation the following January of why such portentous events never occurred. Progress is often a path to greater complications and sorrows.

A major fallacy in liberal thinking is the "essential goodness of the human race." God's word says, " ... *there is none who does good, there is not even one.*" (Romans 3:12). The natural inclination of man is to do that which is contrary to the word of God. We have a written history of mankind for thousands of years and while there has been great technological change, nothing universal has changed in man's attitude toward his brothers or the things his brothers have.

There is always a war going on somewhere. There is unjust imprisonment, persecution, torture, deprivation, murder, and in some cases, annihilation of whole groups of people. Even in so-called civilized countries such as America, we need thousands upon thousands of laws to deal with the constant theft, deception and general dishonesty. Remove the enforcement of such laws and we readily see what happens to our civilized society as demonstrated by the social and race riots of the past fifty years. If the human race is essentially good, where is the evidence?

Any human government that does not include and honor the God of the Christian Bible is doomed to failure. What civilized country has been in existence with the same form of government for more than a few hundred years? What system of government in any country has existed since the time of Adam? History is a tale of the rise and fall of one sinful government after another

Freedom to fall short

The American system has too many allowances for failure. The irony of that is found in our strong assertion of freedom and civil rights. When people have the freedom and personal right to do as they please, without responsibility, there are no barriers against evil. In a land where people are granted the right to sin, ungodliness will become the norm.

We do not have the right to sin, no matter what the liberal philosophers say. If God granted us the right to sin, how then could He punish us for exercising a God-given right? Chastisement for sin would be unjust. There would be no need for a final judgment, or the lake of fire.

Abolishing punishment is the prevailing quest in America today. If Satan can direct our minds to accept that, then we can also expect no punishment from God. That is why criminal justice is becoming a thing of the past. Evil-doers are excused, or given a token punishment, working toward the time when the Satanically inspired liberal agenda will fully eliminate the current penal code. Punishment will only be doled out upon the godly by the elite ungodly.

The American system has lasted this long because the country is so big, geographically, taking over 100 years to settle. Also, the continual technological advances and the large wars kept us preoccupied, but, with the secure, easy life of the second half of the twentieth century, and the newly discovered government entitlements, too much emphasis is on self and having every need met. We have discarded personal responsibility and have become completely dependent upon the modern social-political-economic state of affairs. Throwing off the yoke of this form of slavery would be excessively traumatic for most Americans.

A two-party nightmare

The two-party political system holds us fast. It is Satan's best tool for bringing down what started out as a Christian nation. The political machinery of the Democratic and Republican parties has created systems giving them a political monopoly whereby no one outside of those parties has a chance of getting elected to State or National office. You serve the party or you don't serve at all.

Sometimes, as in the Presidential election of 2008, we have to hold our noses and vote for the lesser of the two evils, but if I do that, I'm still voting for evil. If I am to choose between two ungodly candidates, I might as well get away from both parties and vote for an ungodly candidate of a third-party. Such action causes the conservative party supporters to admonish me for wasting my vote and helping the liberal to win but they have no explanation as to how the liberal candidate won in the '96 and '08 elections after I voted for their supposedly conservative candidate.

If enough people voted for a third-party candidate perhaps the politicians of the two major parties would really get the message and change their ways. Allowing the Democrats or Republicans to continue governing as they do will never get us out of this mess. And, allowing them to serve a lifetime in office is a sure path to disaster.

Politics has become a career, which opens the door for corruption of a great magnitude. Politicians are full of lies and deception, speaking words and doing deeds with only one purpose in mind: getting reelected. It should be a secret to no one that politicians take as much of our money as possible to buy the votes necessary for reelection through pork-barrel spending.

This wickedness will not end as long as one can get reelected for life. Term limits are in place for the President; they should be also for senators and representatives. Congressmen should only be paid for the days Congress is in session and that daily amount should be no more than $200. Dormitories with a cafeteria should be provided at the capitol for living quarters during congressional sessions to eliminate the cost of private housing and the necessity of high salaries. Since it is only the business of Congress to make or repeal laws, huge staffs should be unnecessary.

They should be required to pay for their medical insurance as do the senior citizens, and there should be no retirement benefits for any government office holder. In the least, voters should not reelect anyone to more than two consecutive terms of office.

Even if the political mindset does change in the coming elections it might be too late, as foreign investors won't allow our economy to be in our control. In the near future we will have no fuel or food. Money will be worthless, as there will be nothing to buy. The irresponsible citizens will turn to looting and anarchy. Foreign military powers such as China, Iran, Russia, and North Korea might seize the opportunity to totally eliminate the American super power once and for all and assert their own dominance upon the world.

An apocalyptic event is drawing near for America. It will be God's judgment, as we are forced to drink a bitter cup. Just as individuals and nations have writhed in agony through the centuries in a bitter ending of a sweet beginning, we may be destined for much of the same as we continue to swallow that sweet little book of bad ideas in the form of atheism, feminism, animal rights, environmentalism, education, government, and abortion.

The fact is we have already swallowed much of it and are beginning to feel the symptoms of a grave illness. Our national leaders are prescribing pain killers that are numbing our senses but doing nothing to treat the problem. As sick as we are, still, no one wants to even talk about the only sure cure, which is to repent as a nation and recognize Jesus Christ as the only remedy for sin.

Every time Israel engaged in repentance God's forgiveness and blessing followed. When they fell away, God's wrath fell upon them.

Sometimes, the worst tasting medicine is the best one. It takes courage to realize that and ingest it.

Chapter Two

ATHEISM

A Suggestion to Mankind that there is no God

God's plan of salvation is faith-based. Hebrews 11:6 says, "And without faith it is impossible to please Him, for he who comes to God must believe that He is, and that He is a rewarder of those who seek Him." God's purpose is to save men through Jesus Christ, as in John 6:29. " ... This is the work of God, that you believe in Him whom He has sent." Jesus is the one who was sent.

Satan's purpose is to draw mankind away from God. The easiest and most obvious method of doing that is to get mankind to believe that there is no God. If he can eliminate that required faith in an unseen God from the mind of a man, he will control that man and his fate.

In the second millenium of the human race Satan had virtually succeeded in removing thoughts of God from the people of the Old Testament world. That is evident by reading Genesis 6:12. *"And God* looked on the earth, and behold, it was corrupt; for all flesh had corrupted their way upon the earth." In the next verse He tells Noah that He is about to destroy all flesh, "... the end of all flesh has come before Me ...," but note the reason.

It isn't for merely not believing in Him, but, "... for the earth is filled with violence because of them ... " (Genesis 6:13). Corruption is always the result among a people who have no faith in God and it often leads to violence. Yet, today, those who are being blindly led by Satan reject a God of peace, the only source of true peace, trusting in the wisdom of men to solve the problems of the world. There has been no world peace since Cain killed Abel and there is not the slightest evidence today of world peace becoming a reality through the efforts of men.

The people of Noah's time refused to acknowledge God and His power over all the earth. Noah was the only man who still believed in God, thereby being the only man who heard from God. What he heard was that God was going to destroy all life by means of a great flood and he was to build an ark in which his family would have refuge.

Satan has encouraged the atheists to believe there is no God. If there is no God, there is no judgment after death. If there is no judgment, there is no need of a Savior. The atheists will make false accusations against believers, twist the truth, spread their deception through willing channels, demand an equal hearing, be totally intolerant of any who express faith in God, demonstrate their dislike of Christianity through word and deed, and restrict the free expression of faith by encouraging liberal judges to rule against any public expression of faith in God.

False Accusations

People who turn from the word of God are described in the Bible as fools. Fools are easily deceived and are easy prey for the great deceiver, Satan. Psalm 14:1 reads, *The fool has said in his heart, "There is no God."* Such folks are not called fools because of any clown-like mental deficiency but because of their perverse perception of morality.

The middle part of that verse explains. *They are corrupt, they have committed abominable deeds;* verifying that godlessness breeds corruption. And the end of verse one says, *there is no one who does good.* The atheists' greatest achievement is negative: removing the only moral standard we have as our guide. What hope is there for a people who succumb to such false teaching, who choose to turn off the light and live in darkness?

The apostle Peter spoke of such people in II Peter 2:10. *and especially those who indulge the flesh in its corrupt desires and despise authority. Daring, self-willed, they do not tremble when they revile angelic majesties.* He describes them as "… *reviling where they have no knowledge …* " (v. 12) and, "… *enticing unstable souls …* " (v. 14).

The atheist has no knowledge or understanding of God's eternal purpose and does not comprehend the major theme of the Bible. That does not prevent him from spending much time arguing that which he does not understand and that which he claims to be nothing at all. Imagine what sort of person would spend his life arguing about nothing. Is it any wonder God sees him as a fool?

Another applicable passage is from I Timothy 1:3-7. *As I urged you upon my departure for Macedonia, remain on at Ephesus, in order that you may instruct certain men not to teach strange doctrines, (4) nor to pay attention to myths and endless genealogies, which give rise to mere speculation rather than furthering the administration of God which is by faith. (5) But the goal of our instruction is love from a pure heart and a good conscience and a sincere faith. (6) For some men, straying from these things, have turned aside to fruitless discussion, (7) wanting to be teachers of the Law, even though they do not understand either what they are saying or the matters about which they make confident assertions.*

Paul's warning to the church of Ephesus was of strange doctrines, mere speculation, and fruitless discussion. Any men who brought such offerings did not understand what they were saying. But how are we to know what a "strange doctrine" is? It is any doctrine that does not teach God as the supreme, all-knowing, all-powerful ruler of heaven and earth; Jesus as the Son of God sent to pay the ransom for sin; and a coming judgment at the end of the age. Of course, there are many more details in that theology, revealing God's complete plan for mankind.

Atheists have *exchanged the truth of God for a lie* (Romans 1:25). An apt illustration of how they operate can be found in an account of Daniel's life in Babylon. Daniel, as a youth, was one of the many Jews carried off to captivity by the army of King Nebuchadnezzar to Babylon, the first great world empire, in 605 B.C.

Daniel gained some fame by interpreting a dream for King Nebuchadnezzar and in later years for King Belshazzar, the famous "handwriting on the wall." That particular message from God foretold the end of the Babylonian Empire which occurred that very night and the rise of the Persian Empire, ruled by a man named Darius.

Daniel, chapter 6, relates how King Darius saw something valuable in Daniel so he appointed him as one of three commissioners over the whole country. It was their job to protect the king's interests, and Daniel, because of his "extraordinary spirit," distinguished himself among the others, resulting in the other two commissioners and the 120 satraps (assistants to the king) to become jealous and plot the demise of Daniel.

Verse four of chapter six explains how they ... *began trying to find a ground of accusation against Daniel in regard to government affairs; but they could find no ground of accusation or evidence of corruption, inasmuch as he was faithful, and no negligence or corruption was to be found in him.* That's exactly how such people operate today.

The atheist busybodies, not content with allowing folks to freely exercise their religion as the constitution allows, work diligently to find some part of government that will put the clamps on those judgmental Christians. Even though the atheist claims the right of "religious" expression for himself, there is no such tolerance for Christianity. However, since there is no real law against the public display of religion, the only avenue of suppression for the atheist is through liberal judges and the ACLU, who use the false claim of separation of church and state as the instrument of false accusation, not understanding that they are operating as instruments of the devil.

Well, those tactics were used against Daniel and seemed to be effective as the ungodly men tricked King Darius into establishing a statute that caused any man who made a petition to God (prayer) instead of to the king, be cast into the lions den. That's the motive of such men today – cause people to trust in government rather than God. Satan does his best work through the governments of men.

The phony accusation did cause Daniel to be thrown into the lions den, much to the king's regret, but after a night of hope and prayer, the king saw that God had delivered Daniel from the mouths of the lions. His glad-hearted response was to bring Daniel out and throw the ungodly men (along with their entire families) into the den where they were completely devoured. A similar fate in the lake of fire awaits all who reject the word of God and bring false accusation against His people.

Twisting the Truth

... because of them the way of the truth will be maligned; (II Peter 2:2) That's Peter talking about false teachers who introduce destructive heresies. And Paul chips in, speaking of men ... *who suppress the truth in unrighteousness,* in Romans 1:18, talking about the same kind of people.

The atheist has no written word, as the Christian does, to support his stand. His way around the truth is to deny it. Some may ask the same question about that as Pilate did of Jesus – What is truth? The answer is in John 17:17 where Jesus, while speaking to His Father in Heaven, said, " ... *Thy word is truth."* There you have it. Everything that God says, or does, for that matter, is truth. To deny truth is to deny God, and vice versa.

But what kind of a world would this be without the truth of God? Look at the gross corruption that exists even while the Holy Spirit is active in the world. If He be taken out of the way, what horrors could we expect to come upon us? No doubt, the ones spoken of in the book of Revelation.

The atheist is a form of antichrist as Jesus and the writers of the New Testament warned us about. In II John verse 7 we read, *for many deceivers have gone out into the world, those who do not acknowledge Jesus Christ as coming in the flesh. This is the deceiver and the antichrist.* Daniel 11:32a describes how the great antichrist of the end time will work his deception. *And by smooth words he will turn to godlessness those who act wickedly toward the covenant ...*

The Pharisees, in a dither over their inability to capture Jesus, complained that *"No one of the rulers or Pharisees has believed in Him, has he? But this multitude which does not know the Law is accursed."* (John 7:48, 49).

This is typical thinking on the part of liberal atheists. In their minds, only they understand the truth, and it is the unlearned "multitude" that needs the crutch of religion. The leaders in government and the entertainment world; the college deans and professors; the talking heads of liberal news networks, are above any need for God. They remain in their politically correct attitude of separation of church and state, not giving any credence to the reliability of the gospel.

Stephen, the first martyr, engaged in argument with the Synagogue of the Freedmen, (Acts 6:9), who were Jews from other districts of the middle east that had been captured by Roman conquerors and later freed, with the privileges of Roman citizenship.

The name "Freedmen" was misleading. It was good-sounding, suggesting a well-intentioned group, but they cornered no religious thought and were unable to cope with the wisdom of Stephen. Their response was to induce men to falsely accuse Stephen of blasphemy and have him stoned to death. Truth was not allowed to get in the way of their belief.

There are organizations today with similar sounding names that cause one to think that the organization is an above-board group of people with only the best interests of others at heart, when in reality that activist group is undermining the pillars of biblical truth that this country was founded upon. Study such groups carefully to see if their agenda is in line with God's truth or pursues the way of the antichrist.

Timothy warns against such people. *For the time will come when they will not endure sound doctrine; but wanting to have their ears tickled, they will accumulate for themselves teachers in accordance to their own desires; and will turn away their ears from the truth, and will turn aside to myths.* (II Tim. 4:3, 4).

Those verses are very pertinent to our time where we have cast out the fire and brimstone preacher who warns of God's wrath to come upon the ungodly, in favor of "the gospel of love" message that makes folks feel good about themselves without making a true commitment to the Savior, Jesus Christ.

Rather than accept a God who demands a response from us, the atheist would rather believe in the myth of evolution where all we have to do is be ourselves and everything will work out.

A Contagious Disease

The atheist is a spiritually diseased person. Actually, the Bible says such a person is dead in his sins, but since we see them alive and walking around, it's hard to think of them as being dead. It's much easier to consider them as one who is not whole.

The ungodly words that come out of their mouths are just as deadly as the germs coming from the mouth of a person sick with a contagious disease. Not realizing they are following the ways of their father, Satan, they go about spreading their lies and deception with the danger of causing the uninnoculated (the unsaved) to succumb to the sweet sounding words of freedom from any spiritual responsibility and judgment.

Galatians 5:9 says, *A little leaven leavens the whole lump of dough.* That's the problem of living in a country that grants the constitutional right of free speech. The poisonous, ungodly speech that is permitted does nothing to sustain our moral standards but has been causing a definite drift away from our godly standards, bringing about such actions that we've never seen before and all the while shaking our heads in disbelief and wondering why. I'm not in favor of restricting anyone's right to speak out but we should not be awarding any credibility to the falsehoods of atheism.

Deuteronomy 29:18 speaks of the danger of contamination from false teachers as Moses explained why he was reminding them of how God brought them out of Egypt. *"Lest there shall be among you a man or woman, or family or tribe, whose heart turns away today from the Lord our God, to go and serve the gods of those nations; lest there shall be among you a root bearing poisonous fruit and wormwood."* Any root but the "Root of David" (Rev. 5:5), who is Jesus, is a root bearing poisonous fruit and one that is not to be eaten.

Certain activists with an agenda have recruited prominent people in government and the entertainment world in a low-key suppression of the Christian religion. This began in the 1960s and has been growing like a cancer, with the national media allowing it to go unchecked. They don't even question the validity of the claims made by the atheists of how damaging Christianity is to the American people but readily support the omission of any godly references from our society.

The same thing occurred to the apostle Paul as … *the Jews aroused the devout women of prominence and the leading men of the city, and instigated a persecution against Paul and Barnabas, and drove them out of their district.* (Acts 13:50). A few atheists are using the liberal courts to drive godliness from our ways while we continue to elect ungodly politicians who have no intention of doing anything about it.

The prophet Jeremiah lamented the manner in which the people were blindly following the false teachings of the prophets and priests. *An appalling and horrible thing has happened in the land: the prophets prophesy falsely, and the priests rule on their own authority; and My people love it so! But what will you do at the end of it?* (Jeremiah 5:30, 31)

Equal rights

The big idea behind the push to oust Christianity from our culture is that it isn't fair to folks of other religions and causes much discomfort. Yes, it does cause discomfort because God holds us responsible for the decisions we make and applies penalties for disobedience. But can't the same thing be said of government and all the laws on the books? Government puts more restraints and penalties upon us than God ever did, but what kind of country would we have with no law? And what kind of a country would we have without the Christian influence? The Psalmist asked the same question. *If the foundations are destroyed, what can the righteous do?* (Psalm 11:3)

While demanding the suppression of the Christian's rights, the atheist has no problem at all in demanding his own right to be unoffended. How is it that one person out of one thousand can set the course for the whole group? People are obsessed with equal rights to the point where the rights of whole groups are trampled in order to satisfy the voice of one complaint. We allow ourselves to be herded along as sheep, so as not to be labeled as a racist or homophobe.

The rebels of Israel made their demands of equality to Moses in Num. 16:3, as they said, "… *You have gone far enough, for all the congregation are holy, every one of them, and the Lord is in their midst; so why do you exalt yourselves above the assembly of the Lord?*"

God makes a distinction. There are some that He considers righteous and some that He considers unrighteous. Jesus is the dividing line; so, if the atheist can eliminate God, he doesn't have to deal with Jesus.

The atheist is not entirely irreligious -- only toward Christianity. The inner man is not a vacuum. Everyone has some sort of belief that they rely on; some code of life that they follow. Whatever it is, God sees it as a form of idol worship since it doesn't involve Him. Through the prophet Ezekiel God warned the Israelites to not worship anything but Him. *"And what comes into your mind will not come about, when you say: 'We will be like the nations, like the tribes of the lands, serving wood and stone.'"* (Ezekiel 20:32)

Intolerance

For this is a rebellious people, false sons, sons who refuse to listen to the instruction of the Lord; who say to the seers, "You must not see visions"; and to the prophets, "You must not prophesy to us what is right, speak to us pleasant words, prophesy illusions. Get out of the way, turn aside from the path, let us hear no more about the Holy One of Israel." (Isaiah 30:9-11).

The intolerance of the liberal left (home of the atheists) is amazing in light of their desire to have everyone treated with equal respect. Their treatment of the Christian community betrays the atheist hypocrisy concerning tolerance.

Remove prayer and bible reading from the schools, don't display the Ten Commandments in a public place, get Christ out of Christmas, remove "under God" from the Pledge of Allegiance, and the list goes on. They don't want to hear the truth of God, and they especially don't want to hear the name of Jesus mentioned anywhere.

The atheists claim the Christian religion is judgmental and offensive. Perhaps they should be glad that we don't declare them to be infidels worthy of death and carry out that declaration. They are lucky to not be living in Israel at the time of Moses, where their demands would have been met with the edge of the sword. Would they be espousing their rights if they lived in a country where Islam was the national religion?

There is no reasoning with such people. Right and wrong have no bearing in their demands. Value to them is being able to shout the loudest and get the most press. Abraham's nephew, Lot, received such treatment at the hands of the men of Sodom as he tried to convince them they were on the wrong track.

But they said, "stand aside." Furthermore, they said, "This one came in as an alien, and already he is acting like a judge; now we will treat you worse than them." (Gen. 19:9).

And in Luke 23:23 we read, *But they were insistent, with loud voices asking that He be crucified. And their voices began to prevail.*

The atheists are very tenacious in their insistence. Any delay in granting their wishes only causes their voices to become more shrill in their attempt to drown out any opposition. Of course, their shrillness is what makes news in the eyes (or ears) of most editors, but their best weapon is the liberal court which often produces a favorable ruling.

Hatred

A common accusation of unbelievers against Christians is that we are a people with much hate for those who do not see things our way. We "hate" anyone who doesn't accept the bible as God's word, and we "hate" anyone who is living in social freedom and having fun. Fact is, we don't hate anyone or anything except sin.

The social freedom of today involves the breaking of all ten of the commandments and everything Jesus said in His sermon on the mount. We're not trying to shove the Bible down anyone's throat; we're merely telling others what the Bible says and how it can be used as a guidebook for life.

True hatred is most often exhibited by the ungodly persons of this world. Compare what a Christian says on any news or talk show with what the unbeliever says and how he says it. It's obvious on which side the hatred lies.

II Corinthians 4:4 says, *in whose case the god of this world has blinded the minds of the unbelieving, that they might not see the light of the gospel of the glory of Christ, who is the image of God.*

The ones *"in whose case"* Paul is speaking are *"those who are perishing,"* as mentioned in verse 3, the unbelievers. The god of this world is Satan, who is the father of all unbelievers. Read John 8:44 where Jesus tells the unbelieving Jews, *"You are of your father the devil, and you want to do the desires of your father. He was a murderer from the beginning, and does not stand in the truth, because there is no truth in him. Whenever he speaks a lie, he speaks from his own nature; for he is a liar, and the father of lies."*

This is where the lies, deception, and hatred come from. All unbelievers are instruments in the hands of Satan. They are at enmity with God and His people, blinded by the influence of Satan. Romans 1:21 speaks of how " *... they became futile in their speculations, and their* *foolish heart was darkened."* They have abandoned God while trusting in the futility of myths and theories as an anchor for their ship of life, not understanding that such a position will lead to inevitable shipwreck.

Joseph, loved by his father Jacob as Christians are loved by their father God, was hated by his disobedient brothers in much the same way Christians are hated by their unbelieving, disobedient fellow men. In chapter 37 of Genesis, verse 4 tells us that *" … they hated him and could not speak to him on friendly terms."* Try having a friendly conversation about God with an unbeliever and note the disdain and tone of voice.

Joseph's brothers *"were jealous of him,"* (verse 11) touching on a common, but unadmitted attitude from a no-assurance unbeliever toward a confident and content Christian.

Their hatred of Joseph became so great and consuming that *" … they plotted against him to put him to death."* (verse 18). Persecution comes in increments. It starts with dislike and goes on to hateful intolerance, suppression, and eventual eradication. These steps have been taken against bodies of people for various reasons throughout history.

The persecution of the Christian faith in America began in the 1960s and has slowly been gathering momentum. The liberals of our country are more intolerant of us than they are of the radical Muslim terrorists. They defend the imprisoned terrorists, demanding constitutional rights and humane treatment, but won't have anything to say at the time when Christians are shut up behind prison walls. The Satanically inspired hatred will eventually lead to the ultimate form of persecution; the same final solution used by Hitler.

The Christians Will Rule

The word from the secular world is beware of religion; especially the religion of the Christians, for they want to control the lives of everyone else in both thought and deed. Nay, say the Christians; not true. But a little-understood fact, even by many Christians, is that in this instance what the atheists say is true. The leader of the Christian church, Jesus Christ, has already stated that He has overcome the world and will be the only, and final, ruler of this world. Is it any wonder that the ungodly people of this world, the ones whose father is the devil, do not take too kindly to the Christian church?

The atheist belief system is that if God exists at all, He doesn't know everything, or He would tell us. He cannot be everywhere and see everything because too many people get away with too much. He does not control everything, because He is not here to do it. He is not perfect, because He has made too many mistakes. How can such an imperfect God be any good to the people of earth?

In the mind of the atheist, all answers to all problems can be discovered by men, and, if given enough time, mankind will solve all the problems of the human race. So, who needs God? Who wants "God's people" running our lives?

Well, the truth is, this world has been created by God, mankind was an instant and complete act of creation in our recent past, the human race is separated from God by sin, God has provided a solution for that problem, and God will receive those who accept it and judge those who reject it. Only the children of Satan will object to that statement.

And now you can see why the people of futile, perverted beliefs will quickly jump up to shout down those who speak as I do. There can be no acceptance of a religion that shines a light on their ways, exposing their deeds of darkness for what they are. There must be a total, eventual eradication of Christianity to bring peace to the world as they see it. Indeed, the journalist, academic, and politician of the liberal world are all willing to extend the hand of friendship to the murderous, radical Muslim terrorist while using the other hand to hold the pillow of suffocation over the face of Christianity.

Even though the atheist loudly proclaims the right of free speech and expression, regardless of the extent to which it undermines the moral system of our country, such a person will tear away and stomp on those same rights of the Christian without a word of objection being heard from the ruling liberals.

The Christian take-over will come about, but only after great tribulation of the world at the end of the age, whenever that is. And what will the anti-Christian's position be at that time? If he survives the chaos of the final few years, he will be living in a theocratic Christian world. How awful for him.

He will have to put up with the Christian ruler, that Jesus, ruling what's left of the world, with Christians serving as overseers. There will be no ACLU lawyer jumping to his defense, no liberal judge with whom to file an appeal. He will abide by the Christian rules.

Yes, the poor atheist will be forced to live in a time of peace and harmony. There will be no breaking of the commandments like murder, theft, or adultery. There will be no war, no energy problems, no want of any kind. There will be no democracies, dictatorships or repressive tyrants. There will be no first-, second- or third-world countries. It will be a theocracy, ruled by the head of the Christian church, Jesus. Imagine that. Those Christians, forcing peace and prosperity on the world.

When Christians assume control of the world it won't be because they went to war against the other religions of the world. They will continue to be beaten down awhile until it gets to the point where all life is in peril, and at that point God will intervene by sending the leader of the Christians back to this world in glorified bodily form. Jesus and the Christians will rule.

In the meantime, here is some direction from God's word.

> Daniel 11:32b *... but the people who know their God will display strength and take action.*
>
> Romans 16:17 *now I urge you, brethren, keep your eye on those who cause dissensions and hindrances contrary to the teaching which you learned, and turn away from them.*
>
> Colossians 2:8 *See to it that no one takes you captive through philosophy and empty deception, according to the tradition of men, according to the elementary principles of the world, rather than according to Christ.*
>
> Proverbs 16:3 *Commit your works to the Lord, and your plans will be established.*

Do not allow the sweet-tasting freedom of atheism to bring about the bitter requirements of accountability to God.

Chapter Three

FEMINISM

Takes away the Masculine Authority of God

Since the feminist movement is against any male dominance it is only natural that the movement would attack the gender details of the Bible where all of the references to God are male, the men were the heads of all households, and women had little standing. Feminism is nothing but a form of rebellion against the principles of godly living, so we should not be surprised that the rebelliousness carries directly to God.

God

By claiming that it is a female god who rules heaven and earth, feminism is a direct violation of the first commandment: *"You shall have no other gods before me."* (Exodus 20:3) God inspired the men of old to write the holy scriptures and it isn't likely that He would have allowed them to make the mistake of incorrect gender usage. The writings refer to God as a male because He is using that form to illustrate His relationship with the human race. Any god but a male god is a false god.

But does God really have a gender? It suits His purpose for us to see Him as male, but when we consider the attributes of God – omnipotent, omniscient, omnipresent, can we assign a true gender to Him?

At the burning bush, God delivered the famous "I AM" statement to Moses, saying, *"I AM WHO I AM,"* (Exodus 3:14). A further explanation says, *"I am the Alpha and the Omega," says the Lord God, "who is and who was and who is to come, the Almighty."* (Revelation 1:8).

If there is a person who was not created, but has always existed, and always will exist, and has the power to simply speak things into existence, what need would there be for procreation? Why would that person need a particular gender as we know it?

There is no reference to any being in heaven (angels, elders, creatures, cherubim, seraphim) as being female. In Luke 20:34-36 Jesus said that people who enter heaven will no longer be involved in the marriage relationship, *"for they are like angels."* Apparently, there is no gender among heavenly creatures since there is no death and no need for birth.

God is really not male or female. He simply "is." Gender is for the humans. Since Adam was first, and called a male, God has been denoted as male, since He has always been first. Giving God the female connotation is putting God in a secondary position, like Eve, which is a violation of the first commandment.

Except for extremely rare instances, every living organism on earth is male or female and a joining of the two sexes is necessary for continuation of the species. It's a completely natural concept for us and any other arrangement like one sex or even three sexes would be considered as weird. But God, in His omnipotence, could have set up the human race with any sexual process and any number of genders He desired. So why did He create male and female? It fit His eternal purpose, which is to demonstrate His perfect justice.

God created two sexes in order to show a likeness to His relationship with mankind. There is a passage in Jeremiah where God spoke of how Israel broke the old covenant but He would bring a new covenant. In

31:32, while talking about the breaking of the old covenant, God says, " ... *although I was a husband to them ...* "

In Isaiah 54:5, 6 God said, *"For your husband is your Maker,"* and *"For the Lord has called you, like a wife ... "* That was His relationship with Israel; He was the husband, Israel was the wife.

A husband and wife are to have the same type of relationship as God and man. The husband is to be head of the household and provide and care for the woman just as God is the head of the relationship and provides everything man needs.

Adam wasn't the first to sin because God wouldn't have sinned. In the God-man relationship man is the weaker of the two. The woman was created second, as man came after God, and in some ways, the woman is weaker than the man. God provides for man; man is to be obedient to God. Man is to provide for woman; woman is to be obedient to man. And that's the rub for the feminists.

In an ideal, godly relationship, the male-female system works fine, but remove godliness from either one and there will be no fulfillment or obedience. Godly instruction on that matter can be found in I Corinthians 7:1-16 and in Ephesians 5:22-33 and 6:1-4. Feminism is an ungodly movement inspired by Satan to destroy the man-woman relationship in the hope of further disrupting God's plan for mankind. Sweet in the mouth, bitter in the belly.

Jesus

If the feminist assertion that God is a woman is true, and women do all things better than men, why didn't that female god send her daughter to be the savior of the world? Since women are much more compassionate than men, wouldn't it have made sense to send a more caring savior? Would the Jews have crucified that sweet girl? Ah, sticky problem there, what with that business about blood sacrifice and all, like, no remission of sins without the shedding of blood.

Maybe she decided that's why it would be better to send her son. He would bear up a little better on the cross. Of course, that would be a slap in the feminist face, admitting that son could do a better job than daughter. The only recourse for that embarrassment would be to question whether a savior was sent at all? Yes, that would be more in line with the ungodly feminist thinking.

You see, since a female god would be very compassionate and not send anyone to hell except for maybe the vilest criminals who committed their crimes against women, there would be no need for a savior and that brutal, manly blood stuff. That's the kind of thinking Satan likes to hear, but automatic forgiveness for all would cancel the justice of God and in no way would carry out God's eternal purpose in Jesus Christ.

Feminism is the same as atheism since it produces the same result. If they insist that God is a woman, then either Jesus was a liar or those who wrote about Him were liars, which puts the Bible in a questionable light. If I can't believe some of it, how can I believe any of it? I may as well not believe anything, as the atheists.

The fact is, God presents Himself to us as male, and Jesus, along with the New Testament writers verifies that truth. The apostle Paul, while explaining the qualifications of Christ as high priest, quoted scripture concerning the first coming by saying, *"Thou art My Son, today I have begotten thee;"* (Hebrews 5:5) That's a statement that leaves no doubt that Jesus lived on earth as the son of God, and God also said in Matthew 3:17, *"This is My beloved Son, in whom I am well-pleased."*

While Jesus was still a youth he asked his parents, *"Did you not know that I had to be in My Father's house?"* (Luke 2:49) Throughout the gospels He referred to His "Father in Heaven" without giving any occasion to think that God might be a woman.

John the Baptist explained to the Jews that he was not the Christ, and referring to Jesus and the church he said, *"He who has the bride is the bridegroom;"* (John 3:29) meaning that Jesus and the church would be like husband and wife.

In II Corinthians 11:2 the apostle Paul tells the church, *... for I betrothed you to one husband, that to Christ I might present you as a pure virgin.* In God's eyes the church is as a female and Christ is as the male.

The Bible carries the analogy all the way through as it says, *Blessed are those who are invited to the marriage supper of the Lamb.* (Revelation 19:9) One of the pictures of Jesus is as a lamb, since He was the ultimate blood sacrifice. This view in Revelation shows the bridegroom, Jesus, celebrating His wedding with His bride, the church.

In Rev. 21:9 an angel says to John, *"Come here, I shall show you the bride, the wife of the Lamb."* Then John saw the new Jerusalem coming down from heaven, whose inhabitants are to be, ... *only those whose names are written in the Lamb's book of life.* (Rev. 21:27)

After seeing God likening Himself as the husband of Old Testament Israel we can now see Jesus doing the same as husband of the New Testament Church, a role model for conduct of husband and wife.

Husbands and Wives

Ephesians 5:22 reads, *Wives, be subject to your own husbands, as to the Lord.* Feminists don't want to be subject to anyone for any reason. They equate "subjection" with slavery because they are looking at it from Satan's point of view, but a closer study of this passage reveals instruction for the husband as well, and even for the children of the family.

Keep in mind, as mentioned earlier, that a marriage works as the Bible intends only if both parties show evidence of godliness. A woman in subjection to an ungodly man may well be treated badly, and a man with an unbelieving wife will find it difficult to serve as head of the household. This is why young people should take great care in choosing their mate for life. Disregarding a person's spiritual acclimation for the sake of other seemingly favorable qualities can be disastrous in later years.

Paul warns against being *bound together with unbelievers* in II Corinthians 6:14, a warning that applies to any type of relationship, be it business or marriage. An equally unfavorable situation can occur when neither man or woman are Christians when married but one of them changes in that respect later in life. Instructions for such a situation can be found in I Corinthians 7:10-16, which all men and women would do well to read. Such problems can be troublesome, requiring much prayer and patience, but take refuge in the truth that " ... *with God, all things are possible."* (Matt. 19:26)

The popular culture of personal freedom and individual rights promotes "doing your own thing" without any worry of rejection or recrimination, but we are deluged with examples of how individual action affects others. The notion that we deserve this or that, or are entitled to live as we choose is another deception of Satan whom Jesus said was a liar and a deceiver from the beginning. That's where the cause and effect of behavior started – in the beginning, in the garden of Eden.

Eve may complain long and loud of her "second" status and general misfortune in the garden, but she knew the rules, whether hearing directly from God or secondhand from Adam, because when questioned by the deceiver, she acknowledged that awareness by saying, *"but from the fruit of the tree which is in the middle of the garden, God has said, 'you shall not eat from it or touch it, lest you die.'"* (Genesis 3:3)

She made her choice and convinced Adam to follow suit, thereby bringing an effect upon all women just as Adam did upon all mankind. One of the basic laws of God's creation is that like begets like. Sinful parents conceived sinful children and that has been a curse upon the human race ever since. So much for the assumption that whatever I do is my business and only affects me.

The fact is, God created Eve second. I Corinthians 11:9 says, *for indeed man was not created for the woman's sake, but woman for the man's sake.* Besides that fact it is important for man and woman to both understand verse 12 of that passage which reads, *for as the woman originates from the man, so also the man has his birth through the woman; and all things originate from God.*

After Eve's disobedience, God pronounced her fate and the fate of all women thereafter, by saying, "... *I will greatly multiply your pain in childbirth, in pain you shall bring forth children; yet your desire shall be for your husband, and he shall rule over you.*" (Genesis 3:16)

It doesn't matter whether a woman likes that or not, just as it doesn't matter whether a man likes being born with original sin or not. It is a fact of this world, and any refusal of acceptance is direct rebellion against God. Women may go through their entire life in denial of what God ordained, but in the end what will they do? There is still the moment after this life when it will be necessary to deal with God face to face, a God who changes not. What He said in the beginning will carry through to the end. No matter how shrill or well-versed in human law those ladies are, they will be defenseless in His presence.

Family

Feminism has aided the newfound social entitlement system in destroying the family. But, since family was the first institution God created, it's not surprising that a major attack would come from ungodly feminism.

In the scriptures mentioned earlier, and other places like Proverbs, God clearly states the place and purpose of men, women, and children in the family. Those are the components ordained by God. Any single-parent family that comes about by choice does not comply with God's plan for mankind.

There are cases where some spouses may end up as single parents through no fault of their own, such as death, incarceration for criminal activity, physical abuse, or unfaithfulness, but, providing the remaining spouse is a faithful child of God, His grace will be upon that house and will bless as needed.

Feminists would have us believe and accept the chosen, single-parent household as a place of normality, not requiring the presence of a father for the children. While God is perfect in all His ways and has every quality necessary for parenting Israel, the church, and individuals, neither man nor woman alone have all the qualities needed to provide the example for, and nurturing of, children.

Any parent, man or woman, who puts career ahead of family is doing a great disservice to that structure. On any list of priorities, God has to come first. All life and sustenance comes from God, to say nothing of the great premium of eternal life. Any attempt to go through this life without God's blessing is a foolish attempt beyond measure.

On occasion, a mother may find it necessary to work outside the home due to an unfortunate happening, but great care should be taken in determining the reasons for going to work. It has often been said that God works in strange ways, but we need to be sure that it is His way we are following, and not our own worldly desires. That can only be determined by searching the scriptures and prayer.

A woman who places greater value on her career than on her family is a woman going the way of the ungodly. Such a woman cannot be in a right relationship with God, thereby nullifying her credibility. A woman who rebels against her husband because of worldly desires is rebelling against God.

God gave woman to man as a helpmate. Man is instructed to *Enjoy life with the woman whom you love all the days of your fleeting life which He has given to you under the sun; for this is your reward in life, and in your toil in which you have labored under the sun;* (Ecclesiastes 9:9)

When God comes first for both individuals, such an arrangement is a blessing for both. When a woman decides to taste the sweet fruit of feminism, her rebellion against God is sure to be followed with bitterness.

Homosexuality

Another attack on the traditional family is from the homosexual community. Homosexuality is an unnatural, immoral sexual orientation that Satan has promoted with the intention of destroying the illustration of Christ's union with the church, which is only one more way to alienate man from God. There are numerous references in the Bible that denounce the practice but nowhere can be found an occasion where it is encouraged or condoned.

In Romans 1:26-27, we find an unarguable statement concerning homosexuality. *For this reason God gave them over to degrading passions; for their women exchanged the natural function for that which is unnatural, and in the same way also the men abandoned the natural function of the woman and burned in their desire toward one another, men with men committing indecent acts and receiving in their own persons the due penalty of their error.*

Such men and women have turned away from worshipping the God of truth who wants to adopt them as His children. Rather than give glory to God through Jesus Christ, they choose to glorify the human body and pursue the pleasures of the flesh.

If a homosexual excuses his actions by using the "gene theory," he is placing God in the position of condemning what He created. God would certainly not condemn an uncontrollable human trait in His word. God only holds us responsible for the way we think and the choices we make – not for the physical condition of the human body we are born with.

That particular sexual preference is not an uncontrollable trait. While genetic design does determine the physical makeup and condition of a body, it does not control tendencies, or the way a person thinks about anything. God has given man a spirit that is not subject to the flesh. It's a matter of choice. Choose God or Satan; good or evil; one way or another.

In Genesis 1:27 God's word says ... *male and female He created them.* Genesis 2:20 says, ... *but for Adam there was not found a helper suitable for him*. Why did God create a woman for Adam? Because with two men He could not have said, *"Be fruitful and multiply ... "* (1:28) The most obvious point of the unnaturalness of homosexuality is the inability to become one flesh and bear children.

Another way in which the lifestyle is being granted cultural acceptance is in sex changes. Due to the Satanic deception that men and women can be born into the wrong type of body (sexually) they are correcting the problem by having an operation that changes the sex organs to their preference. What does God think about that? An unmistakable answer appears in Deuteronomy 23:1. *No one who is emasculated, or has his male organ cut off, shall enter the assembly of the Lord."* I guess we could also add that well-known phrase from the marriage ceremony, "What God has joined together, let no man put asunder."

Any surgery involving sex change is nothing more than mutilation, but primarily a shaken fist in the face of God by a defiant child of Satan

The family is God's most sacred institution and homosexuality is a direct affront to the integrity of that group. A family with two men or two women as the "parents" is like a body with two left arms. The second man cannot take the place of a mother, and the second woman cannot take the place of a father. Men and women are different, with different attitudes and different traits. The children of same-sex parents are being short-changed and will grow to adulthood with a skewed perception of what life should be.

Avowed homosexuals can be found in political office, the entertainment world, and the church pulpit, completing a major infiltration by Satan. Ungodly, sympathizing members of the news media love to parade them before us, attempting to make the case for the acceptance of that lifestyle, but woe to anyone who speaks adversely of that sin. Free speech is claimed by the ungodly liberal agenda but vicious attack is brought upon anyone with a godly point of view, labeling them as hate mongers, though it is the liberals who hate the ways of God.

In our country people are free to live however they want to live, within the laws of the land, but when they choose to live in a way that is against the natural truth and morality of God, they have no right to force their way upon others or expect others to accept the way of their choice.

The male-female relationship is exhibited between God and Israel in the Old Testament and Jesus and the Church in the New Testament. The denial of traditional (biblical) relationships between men and women and the acceptance of same-sex relationships is a subtle rejection of Jesus and the Church.

God's offer of forgiveness of sin and the gift of eternal life is extended to all. Except for the sin of blasphemy against the Holy Spirit (Matthew 12:31) God will forgive any sin, including homosexuality. Upon receiving forgiveness a person is expected to "go, and sin no more," but since the spirit is willing and the flesh is weak, few are those who are able to accomplish that. We are to no longer "practice" sin, which is a regular, continual engagement in ungodliness, but to walk in the spirit. When we fail in our resistance to sin, we are to hate it as much as God does, and immediately confess and turn away from it.

Salvation is based on the work of Christ on the cross. In its simplest form, it is granted to anyone who believes God sent Jesus to be the Savior of the world. *"For this is the will of My Father, that everyone who beholds the Son and believes in Him, may have eternal life; and I Myself will raise him up on the last day."* (John 6:40)

Chapter Four

ANIMAL RIGHTS

Removes the Fact of being Created in God's Image

So far we have seen how Satan has used atheism to suggest that there is no God; feminism, to take away the masculine authority of God; homosexuality, to destroy the illustration of Christ's union with the church, and now, he uses the animal rights activists to remove the fact of man being created in God's image; a fact that places man in a superior position to animals.

Although there have been few shining moments in history, mankind is God's jewel of the earth. The earth was created as a place where God could carry out His eternal purpose through Jesus Christ, using man as the object through which He could display His manifold wisdom to all the inhabitants of heaven.

All other life forms, both plant and animal, were created for man's use and were placed in subjection to him. Since the ungodly liberals are only in favor of subjection to their beliefs they make every attempt to remove other granted authority, whether it be of God or man and place it where they will.

The animal rights activists are attempting to raise the animal life of earth to a position of "rightful ownership" and consider mankind as an aberration, detrimental to the well-being of animals. The raising of the worth of animals is contrary to God's word and brings about the lowering of the worth of mankind. The ungodly activists are doing the work of Satan, their father, very well, but shouldn't the promoters of self-esteem be concerned about the reversal of mankind's position (putting us on a level with animals) and what effect it might have on our psyche? Ah, another example of liberal hypocrisy.

Image of God

This is the book of the generations of Adam. In the day when God created man, He made him in the likeness of God. He created them male and female, and He blessed them and named them Man in the day when they were created. (Genesis 5:1, 2)

There are animal-like creatures in heaven (eagle, lion, calf) whose purpose it is to serve and worship God before the throne. (see Revelation 4:7, 8) The creatures of the earth are here to serve man; they are not on equal footing with man.

While man is the only creature on earth that has been created "in the image of God," all animal life (which includes man) is created by receiving "a spirit" from God. Psalm 104:29, 30, in describing the state of animals, gives evidence of that. *Thou dost hide Thy face, they are dismayed; Thou dost take away their spirit, they expire, and return to their dust. Thou dost send forth Thy Spirit, they are created; and Thou dost renew the face of the ground.*

Job 34:14, 15 adds, *If He should determine to do so, if He should gather to Himself His spirit and His breath, all flesh would perish together, and man would return to dust.* "All flesh" would include animals with man.

Well, it sounds like animals are on equal footing with man but that is only in terms of fleshly creation and demise. All receive the spirit of life when created and give it up upon expiration. Man was given an intellect that was withheld from the animals, giving him a similarity to God that no animal has possessed. The creation account in Genesis, chapter 1; the judgment after the fall in chapter 3; the command to post-flood Noah in chapter 9; all speak of the proper position of animal life on earth, which is lower than that of man.

Different Flesh

I Corinthians 15:39, in discussing the resurrection, says, *All flesh is not the same flesh, but there is one flesh of men, and another flesh of beasts, and another flesh of birds, and another of fish.*

Contrary to what the atheists of biology, archeology, geology, and the promoters of evolution say, God created animal life "after their kind," and except for occasional mutations that go nowhere, men, beasts, birds, and fish were created as they are and remain as they are.

In the creation account of Genesis chapter one, God created man on the sixth day. Everything else was created prior to that in preparation for the advent of man. As for the animals, God told man to "... *rule over the fish of the sea and over the birds of the sky, and over every living thing that moves on the earth.*" (Gen. 1:28) No animal flesh was placed on equal footing with, or over, mankind.

In the book of Jeremiah we read of an account where God tells the allies of Judah that He is giving all the nations of that part of the world to King Nebuchadnezzar of Babylon, and, "... *I have given him also the wild animals of the field to serve him.*" (Jeremiah 27:6) The animals were available to the King and probably to any of his subjects, for whatever the need. It was so from the beginning.

Immediately after the fall, provision was made for Adam and Eve, by God. When the first pair of humans ... *knew that they were naked,* (Gen. 3:7) they tried to cover themselves by the use of fig leaves, but God, in His infinite grace, ... *made garments of skin for Adam and his wife, and clothed them.* (Gen. 3:21)

The fig leaves were inadequate so God provided a more lasting covering of skins. And where did the skins come from? There had to have been at least one animal slain by God to provide the covering. It was the first instance of animal death, and the first sacrifice. And, it doesn't take much insight to understand the illustration of the blood sacrifice of the animal covering the nakedness of man, with the blood sacrifice of Jesus covering the sin of man.

God began teaching the work of Jesus in the garden of Eden and carried on that instruction with Cain and Abel, the children of the first pair. When the brothers brought an offering, the Lord had regard for Abel's animal offering, but He had no regard for Cain's offering of "the fruit of the ground."

In Genesis 9:2-4, God instructs Noah on his way of life following the great flood. All beasts, birds, insects, and fish were given into his hand, meaning they were his to use as he saw fit. Every moving thing was given to Noah for food, with the only prohibition being the eating of blood. Man was not to eat the blood of animals because, *"... the life of the flesh is in the blood ..."* and it was used *"... to make atonement for your souls ..."* (Leviticus 17:11)

Some may say that Noah was allowed to eat meat because there was no plant life available right after the flood, and once the crops started growing again there was no reason for him to be a meat eater. In a perfect world that may have been true, but this has never been a perfect world since Adam and Eve were evicted from the garden.

The flood may have washed away some of the natural nutrients of the ground, and with the usual cycle of drought and famine, meat would have been the only nutritional food source available in many times. But most importantly, God never rescinded mankind's permission to use animals at will and eat them for sustenance. Man is to be a good steward of everything God gives him, and that stewardship includes not being abusive to animals. Using those creatures for transportation, protection, or provision is man's right, but it should be carried out with common sense and without abuse.

Exodus 22:19 gives warning against having sex with animals. *"Whoever lies with an animal shall surely be put to death."* Why such a harsh penalty? *"Also you shall not have intercourse with any animal to be defiled with it, nor shall any woman stand before an animal to mate with it; it is a perversion."* (Leviticus 18:23) Much of the venereal disease running rampant in our day had its beginning in sexual intercourse with animals in days gone by. That's the 'why' of the death penalty in that verse. God didn't want His people to be infected from the evil deed of one sinner. If that death penalty had remained in force, perhaps we wouldn't be drinking the bitter cup of sexual disease today. You see, God doesn't want such fraternization with animals because they are of a different flesh. There is nothing about them that puts them on an equal basis with mankind.

Look at what Peter says in his second epistle, 2:12. *"But these, like unreasoning animals, born as creatures of instinct to be captured and killed, reviling where they have no knowledge, will in the destruction of those creatures also be destroyed,"*.

In this passage Peter launches what some might call a diatribe against false teachers as he pulls no punches in delivering the truth of God. In the verse quoted, he compares such people with animals who are "unreasoning" and "creatures of instinct," not being any more knowledgeable than an animal and meeting the same fate as the animals – destruction.

In using Peter as a vehicle of communication, God would not have him use untrue information for an illustration. If Peter spoke of animals as being unreasoning and creatures of instinct, then, that's what they are. They do not have an intellect and are incapable of thinking in logical thought patterns. They react through their God-given instinct and repetitive experience.

However, there are times when an animal may act in a very unusual manner, perhaps in the process of rescuing a human from great danger. With God, all things are possible, and I believe it is entirely possible for Him to temporarily give an animal seemingly human capacity to act in a certain way that would result in deliverance from a negative situation.

In I Kings 17:2-6 you can read of how God had the ravens provide food for Elijah by bringing him bread and meat in the morning and evening. If man can program a computer to "think" in a certain way, surely God can affect the animal brain that He created to respond in a way that is beneficial to a child of God in need.

"Animal rights" is a deception and therefore ungodly, because the word of God gives no rights to the animals. God was able to make a covenant with man because man has the intellect to respond to a covenant. Man can think in a logical sequence and choose different courses of action according to what he sees as beneficial to himself. Of course, because of human nature, man doesn't always choose the best course of action and often does what is contrary to God's law, but still retains the ability to respond to a covenant.

The animal, being a creature of instinct, does not even understand what a covenant is. The person who elevates the animals to the same status as man might as well declare the adding machine of 1910 to have the same importance as the computer of 2010.

The Outcome

"And the wolf will dwell with the lamb, and the leopard will lie down with the kid, and the calf and the young lion and the fatling together; and a little boy will lead them. Also the cow and the bear will graze; their young will lie down together; and the lion will eat straw like the ox. And the nursing child will play by the hole of the cobra, and the weaned child will put his hand on the viper's den. They will not hurt or destroy in all My holy mountain, for the earth will be full of the knowledge of the Lord as the waters cover the sea." (Isaiah 11:6-9)

This is part of a passage that describes life in the millenium; the thousand-year period in which Christ will reign on earth immediately following His second coming. The whole manner of life for all concerned will be different, especially as noted in these verses, for the animals.

They will no longer be food for humans and each other. They will no longer have the fear of man and each other. Survival of the fittest and the rule of the food chain will no longer apply. All animals will have plant life for food (no more meat eaters) just as all mankind will have fruit, vegetables and grain for food, just as it was in the garden of Eden before sin entered the world. How can this be, you ask?

Well, note that I said, "before sin entered the world." Before Adam and Eve sinned, it was a perfect world. When Christ returns and Satan is bound in the pit, the world will be "perfect" once again. The rule of sin will not prevail. The knowledge of the Lord will permeate the earth, causing all creatures to live in harmony. The animals will no longer instinctively eat one another. Their masticating and digestive systems will be restored to their original workings before the era of sin, when they were capable of subsisting on plant life. Remember, with God, all things are possible, and it is His word that says this will come about.

The first commandment says we should have no other gods before us. Animal rights organizations are worshipping the creature instead of the creator. We should not be adjusting our lives due to the whims of a few ungodly people with time on their hands, government funding in their wallets, and politicians in their pockets. Too many liberal activist organizations, whether it is animal rights or environmentalists, are no more than fronts for socialist or communist groups who are trying to destroy America by putting further burdens on individual property rights and our economy.

The right to own property and do with it as you will, regardless of what creature or insect lives there, is the right of an American citizen. Using animal rights and the Endangered Species Act to prevent property owners from exercising their constitutional rights is anti-American and ungodly.

The animal rights activists are pushing an ungodly issue because God's word never gives animals an equivalence to man, but states that only God can bring about an amiable relationship between man and animal. People do well to work toward ending the abuse of animals but are out of step with God when they assign rights to animals; rights that God never gave.

When such ungodly, unrepentant activists stand before God and they have no adequate response to His demand for righteousness, perhaps the words of Job 12:7-10 may be instructive to them. *"But now ask the beasts, and let them teach you; and the birds of the heavens, and let them tell you. Or speak to the earth, and let it teach you; and let the fish of the sea declare to you. Who among all these does not know that the hand of the Lord has done this, in whose hand is the life of every living thing, and the breath of all mankind?"*

Their ungodly works shall be burned up in the purifying fire of God with no one standing to make intercession for them. They shall have their part in the lake of fire with the devil whom they so foolishly followed.

But it doesn't have to be that way. If such folks will repent of their ungodliness, give Him the glory and be transformed by the renewing of their minds, God will receive them as adopted children with all the benefits of salvation through Jesus Christ. After that, everything in God's creation falls into its proper place.

Chapter Five

ENVIRONMENTALISM

Exchanges Worship of God for Worship of the Earth.

There is nothing wrong with wanting a clean place to live, clean air to breathe, and clean water to drink. All people want that, no matter what their political or philosophical beliefs are. The wrongness of environmentalism is when certain groups take it upon themselves to be the caretakers of the Earth, conspiring to have laws passed and regulations put in place that restrict man's rightful use of the property that God gave to him.

Such conspiratory action is rooted in evil (a desire to control people's lives) and encouraged by Satan. The environment has become one of the devil's effective weapons and his instruments, the ungodly liberals, are wielding it mightily. Of course, many uninformed folks on the conservative side have been enabling the forecasters of world-wide ecological disaster to continue in their rantings.

But what purpose would Satan have in promoting radical environmentalism? It's just another step in removing the sovereignty of God from this earth. In order to strengthen the mindset of self-determining man, God's control of the earth must be taken away by convincing people that it is they who hold the balance of nature in their hands.

If environmentalism was accepted by all as it is presented, there would be great change in the lives of Americans. In order to prevent extreme climate change we would experience extreme social and cultural change. Our government would answer to the United Nations; the way we work, travel, eat, and produce would be controlled by the UN regulations on the environment.

While the "emerging" nations would be exempt from the regulations, full application would be in effect in the United States having a devastating result on our economy. History has shown that when a people is in great need, the door is swung open for the dictator, socialist, or communist who is saying the right things and making the best-sounding promises.

When the dust settles, America would be beaten economically, politically, and very likely, militarily. America, the great stronghold of Christianity, would no longer be the beacon of light, holding back the forces of darkness. The ungodly would have full reign to pursue their wicked ways, which fits Satan's purpose.

The current craze of the radical environmentalists is global warming – perhaps the greatest hoax ever perpetrated upon mankind. Since our marvelous communication and travel systems have seemingly shrunk the earth to the point where every place is our back yard, we have now developed the ability to affect the whole earth by simply living on it, or so we are told.

The truth is, we are nothing more than we've ever been – surface-scratchers. A photograph of the earth from the moon doesn't show any evidence that we even live here. More importantly, the Bible does not even suggest that mankind will do itself in through ecological destruction. It does state that it is God who created this earth and causes everything to happen, and when the end does come, it will be the swift and unforeseen action of the hand of God that destroys much life on this planet, not the slow melting of the icecaps.

Any supposed self-annihilation by mankind would put God in the preposterous position of not foreseeing such an event and not having a plan to deal with it. However, there will come a day when mankind is on the verge of self-annihilation through general nastiness toward each other, such as one final battle, but it will be man dying at the hand of man, not mankind being extinguished by catastrophic environmental events. Such events will occur, as noted in Revelation, but will serve the purpose of bringing mankind to the realization that God is in control.

Matthew 24:22, in speaking of the great tribulation, says, *and unless those days had been cut short, no life would have been saved; but for the sake of the elect those days shall be cut short.* God is always in control and He has told us exactly how and why this world will come to an end.

Yes, man has polluted this earth, but not from creating material garbage. The whole earth has been corrupted by sin, which is the direct result of man's disobedience to God. This is an "inconvenient truth" for the radical environmentalists who are spreading the lies and deception of Satan, the adversary of God.

The Creator

In the beginning God created the heavens and the earth. (Gen. 1:1) That is the beginning of all the words that God had men write down for us. Before we are told anything about God or His plan for mankind we are told that this entire universe is His creation.

And He is before all things, and in Him all things hold together. (Colossians 1:17) That is one of the powerful truths of the Bible. Scientists, for centuries, have been trying to determine what was the beginning of all things and what is the secret of molecular and atomic physics. It's simple – the power of God. Jesus is the force that holds molecules and atoms together.

That verse in Colossians is embedded in a passage where Paul is explaining the work of Jesus Christ, who apparently is the creative force of the Godhead. Verse 16 of that first chapter says, "*For by Him all things were created, both in the heavens and on earth, visible and invisible, ...* "

The book of Hebrews attests to that by adding, *in these last days has spoken to us in His Son, whom He appointed heir of all things, through whom also He made the world.* (1:2) And, *Thou hast put all things in subjection under His feet.* (2:8)

The writer of Hebrews also tells us that God is in control and has a plan for the heavens and earth in His good time. *"And, Thou, Lord, in the beginning didst lay the foundation of the earth, and the heavens are the works of Thy hands; they will perish, but Thou remainest; and they all will become old as a garment, and as a mantle Thou wilt roll them up; as a garment they will also be changed. But Thou art the same, and Thy years will not come to an end."* (Heb. 1:10-12)

The laws of science are God's laws. Is it any wonder that man has such a hard time understanding them? If this world and all its properties and life came into being through the random acts of evolution there would be no scientific laws governing anything. How could life have developed to this point? Any "life" would be nothing more than an unviable tissue mass, borrowing the language of the abortionist. An unviable tissue mass is on the order of a tumor. A tumor is an aberration. Order does not come from chaos.

The world of science has progressed much in the last 200 years with great technological breakthroughs, but, with all their formulae, their equations and theories, they're still not any closer to knowing where we came from and where we're going.

It is not mankind who controls the seasons and annual weather patterns. Major change in the earth's climate has never been and never will be determined by the actions of man. We're told that our ancestors were cavemen with rudimentary tools and weapons, and that it was in their time that the most dramatic climate changes occurred such as major ice ages. How did that happen? The cavemen weren't driving cars or operating factories. Psalm 74:15-17 tells us who controls the weather and seasons.

Thou didst break open springs and torrents; Thou didst dry up everflowing streams. Thine is the day, Thine is the night; Thou hast prepared the light and the sun. Thou hast established all the boundaries of the earth; Thou hast made summer and winter. Not a hint there of man's effect on the weather.

Perversion

While Jesus was speaking to His Heavenly Father on the eve of His crucifixion, He said to Him, *"Thy word is truth."* (John 17:17) Truth comes only from God, so if one turns away from that truth, he will be living in a world of lies and deception. If one turns away from the truth of God being the creator and sustainer of all things, he is left with the deception of environmentalism.

For the time will come when they will not endure sound doctrine; but wanting to have their ears tickled, they will accumulate for themselves teachers in accordance to their own desires; and will turn away their ears from the truth, and will turn aside to myths. (II Tim. 4:3-4)

There are many folks in the world of politics, journalism, and education who have no use for the word of God. They work hard to replace the problem of sin in the world with manufactured crises, suited to give them prestige and power over the citizens, not realizing they are carrying Satan's water. Putting environmental responsibility on the people, like global warming, is nothing more than a distraction to keep the light of righteousness from shining on their evil deeds of darkness. Global warming caused by man is a devilish deception.

The earth and animal worshippers have perverted the glory of God's creation by giving the ground and the creatures a position never given by God. His word explains in I Corinthians 15:39-41 that everything is of itself, created after its own kind and having no special reason for glorification, including the earth and the cosmic bodies.

All flesh is not the same flesh, but there is one flesh of men, and another flesh of beasts, and another flesh of birds, and another of fish. There are also heavenly bodies and earthly bodies, but the glory of the heavenly is one, and the glory of the earthly is another. There is one glory of the sun, and another glory of the moon, and another glory of the stars; for star differs from star in glory.

Men look past the word of God to the created thing to find the mechanics of creation, much like they would study the materials of a building without considering the architect and the construction company to find whereabouts it came from.

The needs of, and benefits to, the citizenry are secondary to insects and other tiny creatures when it comes to many construction projects and normal use of private land. The tree huggers would rather spare the tree than provide lumber to build homes for those in need of shelter. What do you suppose would happen to our economy if we stopped cutting trees, shut down all oil wells and coal mines, closed any factories that polluted in the least, and stopped driving internal combustion cars?

What would happen to our way of life? We would be under control of a very few people with only evil on their minds.

Another great evil is turning our attention from this earth toward other worlds in the universe where life such as ours might exist. God's eternal purpose is being carried out upon this earth alone, which is where our focus should be. Satan encourages the unbelievers to look to the stars for hope.

Science tells us that there are many planets in this universe like Earth and concludes that there could be many with intelligent life. Even some Christians will ask if there could be life on other planets around a distant star. As mentioned earlier, God's eternal purpose does not require any other planet but Earth, and even tells us the purpose of all other cosmic objects.

Then God said, "Let there be lights in the expanse of the heavens to separate the day from the night, and let them be for signs, and for seasons, and for days and years; and let them be for lights in the expanse of the heavens to give light on the earth"; and it was so. And God made the two great lights, the greater light to govern the day, and the lesser light to govern the night; He made the stars also. And God placed them in the expanse of the heavens to give light on the earth, and to govern the day and the night, and to separate the light from the darkness; and God saw that it was good. (Gen. 1:14-18)

It's clear from that reading that the stars were placed in the heavens "for signs, and for seasons." They are there for the benefit of man; to plant and grow by, to navigate by, to tell time by, and to have a little light at night to take away the deep blackness of space. The stars, in their seemingly unchangeable positions, provide a splendid illustration of the ever-present and unchangeable God. Just as the stars appear to be eternal, God will always be there. Even though there is darkness, Jesus is the light of the world.

Do not look to the stars for an alien messiah who will have all the answers to our problems. Any such manifestations are from the devil. There are only two types of beings – heavenly and earthly. Heavenly angels have made appearances in our world, but not along the lines of the supposed visitors from space. When an angel appears, he delivers his message from God, and that's it. Satan's demons engage in deception and confusion. There is human life on this planet alone and we should not be looking for deliverance from any object or creature, be it earthly or cosmic, wood or stone.

Jeremiah blasted the idolatrous Jews, condemning them for their worship of stone and wood idols. *Who say to a tree, 'You are my father,' and to a stone, 'You gave me birth.' For they have turned their back to Me, and not their face; but in the time of their trouble they will say, 'Arise and save us.'* (2:27)

How could a piece of wood carved into a particular form be a God? How could a piece of stone chiseled into a form have the power of life and death? How could our treatment of the environment determine the issue of eternal life?

When the liberal, radical environmentalists preach their deception they are no different than the Israelites who said, *"we will be like the nations, like the tribes of the lands, serving wood and stone."* (Ezekiel 20:32)

Many people refuse to believe the account of the great flood in Noah's time, of which there is evidence around the world, but jump on the bandwagon of global warming which is speculation without evidence. They use the statistics of periodic climate change to produce a false picture of world-wide doom, rejecting the truth of God but believing the lies of Satan.

They would have us turn away from the godly principles of America to the darkness from which our forefathers ran, centuries ago. We have no business taking up the cultures of other peoples or their ungodly approach to the condition and direction of this world. Satan's work can be found in the United Nations and in the desires of radical leaders of second- and third-world countries.

The story of the Tower of Babel serves warning against any one-world government. Such institutions become self-serving, demanding that the constituents look to them for the handling of all concerns, rather than serving and giving glory to God.

Creation Suffers

The environmentalists tell us the earth is being ruined by mankind, and the ruining is happening because of the way we live. Therein lies the deception of Satan. He is deflecting the source of the ruination from the sin of man in the garden of Eden to our lack of care for our environment today. Any effort on our part to cleanse the earth is futile. The pollution won't be taken away until God does it at the end of this age. We can pick up our garbage but we can't control climatic conditions.

Consider this reading from Isaiah: *Behold, the Lord lays the earth waste, devastates it, distorts its surface, and scatters its inhabitants. And the people will be like the priest, the servant like his master, the maid like her mistress, the buyer like the seller, the lender like the borrower, the creditor like the debtor. The earth will be completely laid waste and completely despoiled, for the Lord has spoken this word. The earth mourns and withers, the world fades and withers, the exalted of the people of the earth fade away. The earth is also polluted by its inhabitants, for they transgressed laws, violated statutes, broke the everlasting covenant. Therefore, a curse devours the earth, and those who live in it are held guilty. Therefore, the inhabitants of the earth are burned, and few men are left.* (24:1-6)

I guess that's why insurance companies call such catastrophic events "an act of God." It is God who brings devastation in response to the disobedience of men. It's clearly because of men violating the laws, statutes, and covenant of God – not because of our working, playing, and use of natural materials. But keep in mind that every disaster of nature is not necessarily God doling out instant retribution upon a sinful group of people. The nature of man has spoiled the nature of earth.

The forces of nature are the forces of God operating according to His laws which were set up at the beginning and afforded mankind a hospitable place to live, especially the garden of Eden. After the willful sin of Adam and Eve, the earth was cursed along with the people, but just as it took a long time for sin to affect the physical condition of man (they lived to be 900 years old during the first millenium) the violent effects of sin, indirectly, upon the earth in the form of volcanoes, earthquakes, hurricanes, tornadoes, and general weather patterns didn't fully come about until after the flood.

Before the flood, during Noah's time, there apparently was a huge canopy of water vapor surrounding the earth, protecting it from the harmful radiation of the sun and producing a greenhouse effect that caused moderate temperatures all over the earth. The seas were much smaller, with the land mass concentrated in one large portion of the globe, reducing the effect of large, world-wide weather patterns.

In Genesis 7:11, the Bible describes what happened. *"In the six hundredth year of Noah's life, in the second month, on the seventeenth day of the month, on the same day all the fountains of the great deep burst open, and the floodgates of the sky were opened."*

At the time of His choosing, God introduced a "monkey wrench" to His creation. What that was and how it happened, we don't know, but we do know that on the same day, all the water under the ground began to be forced to the surface and all the water vapor in the canopy surrounding earth started coming down, continuing for forty days and nights, flooding the entire earth. All of mankind except eight people (Noah's family) were drowned, and all birds and beasts except for the small group that accompanied Noah on the ark, perished.

Following the deluge, conditions on earth were very different. The protective canopy no longer blocked solar radiation, likely causing the fleshly body to wear out much sooner. Earthquakes pushed land up in some places while dropping it in others, forming huge new continents and great oceans. Psalm 104 offers a good description of our world as God intended it, but verses 5-9 tell us specifically what happened after the flood..

He established the earth upon its foundations, so that it will not totter forever and ever. Thou didst cover it with the deep as with a garment; the waters were standing above the mountains. At Thy rebuke they fled; at the sound of Thy thunder they hurried away. The mountains rose; the valleys sank down to the place which Thou didst establish for them. Thou didst set a boundary that they may not pass over; that they may not return to cover the earth.

The different elevations of the continents and the breadth of the vast seas caused temperature differentials which produced a new weather machine, spawning the storms, droughts and seasonal variations that we now experience. And yes, sometimes God uses those things to chastise His people and bring judgment on others.

Verse five is very noteworthy where it speaks of *"the earth upon its foundations,"* and that *"it will not totter forever and ever."* The earth sits on nothing and is hung on nothing. The gravitational pull of the sun and the earth's momentum is its foundation, and those forces keep it "tottering" in its place, always on the verge of flying off into space or crashing into the sun. But note that the verse says God set it in that position so that it will not last forever. Might an intrusion from another object in our solar system cause that delicate balance between sun and earth to go awry? The judgments of Revelation give such an indication.

Trying to save the environment without addressing the root cause of the pollution (a spiritual problem) is futile. The environmentalists talk as though it is only Americans that are ruining the earth, but the Bible tells us it was ruined from the beginning.

For the anxious longing of the creation waits eagerly for the revealing of the sons of God. For the creation was subjected to futility, not of its own will, but because of Him who subjected it, in hope that the creation itself also will be set free from its slavery to corruption into the freedom of the glory of the children of God. For we know that the whole creation groans and suffers the pains of childbirth together until now. (Romans 8:19-22)

The whole creation was set on edge because of sin. After the flood, because of a lack of plant food for awhile, many animals survived as carnivores and have continued in that role, all becoming prey for mankind who survived as a meat eater. The earth is in the throes of inhabitant self-destruction and damaging weather conditions. Those are two things that cannot be changed within the power of mankind.

Knowledge

In Job 12:9-10, the man who suffered great loss challenges his friend to check with the beasts, birds and fish for knowledge of God, and asks the question: *Who among all these does not know that the hand of the Lord has done this, in whose hand is the life of every living thing, and the breath of all mankind?*

If we asked who among men does not know this, the answer would be: all unbelievers, among whom are scientists, teachers, college professors, journalists and political leaders. That bit of information provides great insight into why we are largely a secular society. The trained, educated minds won't allow the "foolishness of religion" to sway the theories and postulations of intellectual thinking.

"Where were you when I laid the foundation of the earth! Tell Me, if you have understanding, who set its measurements, since you know? Or who stretched the line on it? On what were its bases sunk? Or who laid its cornerstone ... " (Job 38:4-6)

God asks these questions of all the educated people of the world. After all of our scientific advancement, our high technology and our heretofore unheard of abilities, we still can't answer those questions because we weren't there to see it done. The geologists and anthropologists look at bones and rocks and make an educated guess as to how old they are, but it is all speculation.

The conditions of cause and effect were entirely different in the beginning from what they are today. The great error of science is in applying the workings and conditions of nature today to the world of thousands of years ago. Why do we expect things to be the same 4,000 years ago as they are today? Why have the science textbooks been updated so often in the last 100 years? Because we have learned more, you say? That's right. We're always finding out we didn't know as much as we thought we did. How unscientific it is to be sure that an unmeasurable event – one that cannot be examined – did or did not happen in a certain way, or did not happen at all.

And notice also in those last verses quoted, the questions all refer to a "who" as the one responsible for the creation. They ask who did it and how did he do it. There is not the slightest hint that this world and all life upon it came into being through random acts of nature, such as the evolutionist proposes.

The liberal bastion is a contradictory one. It contains the "survival of the fittest" evolutionist who believes that is how we arrived at where we are today and it is also the home of the "equal opportunity" pushers. I wouldn't think those two groups would get along at all since equal opportunity has no place in the theory of evolution. If the Darwinist law of survival of the fittest is the liberal religion, wouldn't equal opportunity be blasphemy or sacrilegious?

Just as you do not know the path of the wind and how bones are formed in the womb of the pregnant woman, so you do not know the activity of God who makes all things. (Ecclesiastes 11:5)

Weather forecasting is so inaccurate that conditions cannot be predicted more than a few days in advance. So, how foolish are the detailed predictions about global warming? And, even though we have learned much about DNA, it is still only the hand of God that creates an infant in the womb.

And I saw every work of God, I concluded that man cannot discover the work which has been done under the sun. Even though man should seek laboriously, he will not discover; and though the wise man should say, "I know," he cannot discover. (Ecclesiastes 8:17)

Man does not have the capacity for understanding the work of God's creation. Try as he may, man's attempts are an exercise in futility. There is too much to know and it is much too complicated. What confounds science the most is that all new discoveries only point to the hand of a creator, rather than being a confirmation of their humanistic beliefs.

As we draw nearer to the end of the age more evidence will be discovered and more things learned that will validate the scriptures. All things will come together in Christ, but the increasing evidence of God will only cause the ungodly to shake their fists even more. They won't believe it because they don't want to believe it.

By faith we understand that the worlds were prepared by the word of God, so that what is seen was not made out of things which are visible. (Hebrews 11:3)

The unseen is unacceptable by the world. Just as the unbelieving Jews had to see a sign from Jesus, so the unbelievers of today have to see the tangible evidence. Astronomers cannot believe that something was made from nothing, yet that is what the word of God says. The frightful evidence of the "big bang" is staring them in the face, leaving them with the problem of where that original ball of matter came from. It had to come from nothing, that is, it was spoken into existence by God.

And why would that big bang and resulting expansion of the universe have to be over a period of billions of years? Are not all things possible with God? Could He not have completed it in one day of creation? When you look up at the night sky, the stars and galaxies seem to be frozen in space, but if you were the size of a galaxy, you would see the celestial objects moving and changing at a rapid speed. Remember, things were very different in this universe before the fall of man, and we are seeing things from our tiny, slow perspective.

The scientific theories concerning the past are mere theories because those events were unobserved and cannot be measured. They can only be taken on faith. Science is no different than religion in that respect.

Provision

"While the earth remains, seedtime and harvest, and cold and heat, and summer and winter, and day and night shall not cease." (Genesis 8:22)

That is God's promise to mankind after the great flood. How does that promise fit in with the environmentalists' dire warnings of the earth's destruction at the hands of men? Has God underestimated us? Do we have the power to override the word of God? Is God going to be looking down someday, somewhat perplexed at the way things turned out?

The radical, ungodly environmentalists would have us believe that we can thwart God's eternal purpose. The devilish deception would have us focus on a fraud and not foresee the impending judgment of God upon this world, thereby causing many more souls to become eligible for the lake of fire. Satan is basing his hoped-for victory on numbers, but God will win through righteous action.

And they who dwell in the ends of the earth stand in awe of Thy signs; Thou dost make the dawn and the sunset shout for joy. Thou dost visit the earth, and cause it to overflow; Thou dost greatly enrich it; the stream of God is full of water; Thou dost prepare their grain, for thus Thou dost prepare the earth. Thou dost water its furrows abundantly; Thou dost settle its ridges; Thou dost soften it with showers; Thou dost bless its growth. Thou hast crowned the year with Thy bounty, and Thy paths drip with fatness. The pastures of the wilderness drip, and the hills gird themselves with rejoicing. The meadows are clothed with flocks, and the valleys are covered with grain; they shout for joy, yes, they sing. (Psalm 65:8-13)

God causes the earth to increase its bounty to provide for His obedient people. When we follow the commandments of the Lord, all the work we do upon the earth will be blessed and the earth will respond. There is no worry of environmental pollution under such conditions. God has decreed it.

In Genesis 3:19 God told Adam that *"by the sweat of your face"* he would earn a living on this earth. Nothing would come easy. Man would have to plow the ground, plant the seed, cultivate and harvest it to put bread on his table. He would have to chop wood to build a house for shelter and a fire for warmth. At a later time he would be digging coal for warmth and energy, and drilling for gas and oil for the same reasons.

Adam was told that he would have to work hard to get the things necessary for survival, but God placed everything that was needed in this earth. For as long as man is on this earth there will always be a sufficient supply of land for tilling, and wood, coal, gas, and oil for heating and energy. God knew how much we would need and He put it there. If we are running out of some of these things, then wouldn't that be a sign of the closeness of the end of the age?

Satan uses the manmade value of some of these materials as a method of temptation in wicked individuals. The fact that there is such great concern about the availability of oil in particular around the world, influencing many international decisions, is another sign that we may be nearing the time of Armageddon.

Do not believe that we live on such a fragile earth that our natural movements could set off a chain of uncontrollable, disastrous events. God created this earth as our abode and He has sovereign control of it. When it has served its purpose, He will change it – not us.

Judgment

Whether it be wind, water, fire, or quake there is something happening somewhere as the forces of nature are continually churning the Earth. These forces are providentially used by God to bring blessing, or, as noted in Nahum 1:3-6, judgment. *The Lord is slow to anger and great in power, and the Lord will by no means leave the guilty unpunished. In whirlwind and storm is His way, and clouds are the dust beneath His feet. He rebukes the sea and makes it dry; He dries up all the rivers ... mountains quake because of Him, and the hills dissolve; indeed the earth is upheaved by His presence, the world and all the inhabitants in it. Who can stand before His indignation? Who can endure the burning of His anger: His wrath is poured out like fire, and the rocks are broken up by Him.*

It is more likely to be the hand of a wrathful God behind a great disaster than the burning of fossil fuels by man, but since the atmospheric and geological realms are in continual movement like the gears of a clock, deadly events are going to happen as a natural part of life on Earth.

Besides judgment, God sometimes uses these forces as a form of chastisement to turn His people around, much like the dog nipping at the heels of the sheep to drive them back to the flock. "*I smote you and every work of your hands with blasting wind, mildew, and hail; yet you did not come back to Me,*" declares the Lord. (Haggai 2:17)

There may be some readers who are offended at my description of the radical environmentalists as "ungodly," but consider what the Lord says in Jeremiah 17:5. *Thus says the Lord, "cursed is the man who trusts in mankind and makes flesh his strength, and whose heart turns away from the Lord."*

The people who have set up environmentalism as their religion do not take God's word into account with their theories and pronouncements. In all the speeches, pamphlets, books, and movies, there is a glaring absence of the sovereignty of God. Indeed, none of the issues of the liberal agenda include God in anything, except in the argument about church and state. And since it all is Satanic inspired, why would we expect to see God's side in any of these issues, particularly environmentalism?

Those people have removed God from the picture and altered the place of man on earth to nothing more than an interloper who is messing everything up, and the "natural" world would be better off without him. How can these folks be described in any other way than "ungodly?" What is their solution to the supposed environmental crisis? Turning to God in repentance? No, they're telling us what we need to do to fix the problem, and that's exactly what that verse in Jeremiah 17:5 says.

There are two passages in Isaiah that can be applied to the end of the age. In chapter 13 God declares His judgment on Babylon, but from the wording, we can see that it applies to the end-time "Babylon;" the one spoken of in Revelation.

Behold, the day of the Lord is coming, cruel, with fury and burning anger, to make the land a desolation; and He will exterminate its sinners from it. For the stars of heaven and their constellations will not flash forth their light; the sun will be dark when it rises, and the moon will not shed its light. Thus I will punish the world for its evil, and the wicked for their iniquity; ... (vs. 9-11) *Therefore I shall make the heavens tremble, and the earth will be shaken from its place at the fury of the Lord of hosts in the day of His burning anger.* (vs. 13)

In chapter 24:20 of Isaiah, another passage on the tribulation period at the end of the age, it is said that, *The earth reels to and fro like a drunkard, ...*

The earth being shaken from its place and reeling to and fro could only happen as the result of near contact with another celestial body such as a comet or meteor, as mentioned earlier pertaining to the passage in Psalm 104:5. It may sound like science fiction to some but there are credible institutions who are studying that possibility and what the effects would be. A slight change in orbit could cause a great difference in the amount of heat from the sun, one of the conditions prophesied about the end of the world.

And the second angel sounded, and something like a great mountain burning with fire was thrown into the sea; and a third of the sea became blood; (Rev. 8:8) Could a comet or large meteor come crashing into the earth and also cause a slight change in orbit? Such an event would definitely bring about the conditions predicted by the radical environmentalists, but who, or what, would they list as the cause? They couldn't blame a wayward comet on us, and they certainly wouldn't give glory to God by citing the work of the second trumpeteer of Revelation. Quite a dilemma for those folks -- a crisis with no one to blame.

God is in control and He has told us how He has done things and how He's going to do other things. ... *by the word of God the heavens existed long ago and the earth was formed out of water and by water, through which the world at that time was destroyed, being flooded with water.* (II Peter 3:5-6)

God told us that the present condition of this earth came about because of the great, world-wide flood. The huge amount of water shaped the ocean beds and continents, and developed the weather patterns. And, in verses 7 and 10 of that chapter, Peter tells us how it all ends.

But the present heavens and earth by His word are being reserved for fire, kept for the day of judgment and destruction of ungodly men. But the day of the Lord will come like a thief, in which the heavens will pass away with a roar and the elements will be destroyed with intense heat, and the earth and its works will be burned up.

It doesn't sound like we are going to have any control at all in the demise of this earth, does it? Until the "day of the Lord," life will go on. In Matthew chapter 24, Jesus spoke of the continuation of wars, famines, and earthquakes leading up to the end of the age. There will also be violent storms and minor climate changes.

Every winter is not the same; every summer is not the same; every storm is not of the same intensity. Why shouldn't the climate be warmer or colder in different times? The whole notion of uncontrollable global warming caused by the action of mankind is so preposterous and has become so wearisome that I speak of it only as a warning to Christian folk to not succumb to the devil's lies. For it is he who plants such ungodly notions in the minds of men, and it is his words that we hear from the mouths of the unproductive busybodies. Do not be deceived.

The Outcome

Yes, what about the outcome? Up till now, it doesn't matter who is right – the environmentalist or the Christian, because it sounds like a good news bad news thing. The good news is that the environmentalists are wrong, but the bad news is, the earth is still going to be destroyed some day by a fiery ordeal. Where does that leave us?

Chapter 21 in the book of Revelation tells us that the great ball of fire is not the ultimate end of our life. It speaks of a new heaven and a new earth where the godly people will spend eternity with all needs met by an ever-present God.

It will be the final victory of God with a complete eradication of sin. Satan will have been thrown into the lake of fire, never to come out again, (Rev. 20:10), the ungodly will have met the same fate, (Rev. 20:15), and the earth that was polluted with sin will have been destroyed and completely made over. Fire purifies and cleanses everything.

Do not look to the radical liberals for redemption -- look to Jesus. *"I am the way, and the truth, and the life; no one comes to the Father, but through Me.* (John 14:6)

Chapter Six

EDUCATION

The Liberal Pollution of the Minds of Children

An ancient proverb of Israel said, "*The fathers eat the sour grapes, but the children's teeth are set on edge.*" (Ezekiel 18:2) God told the Israelites in Ezekiel 18:3 that they wouldn't be using that proverb anymore since He judged people for their own sins; not the sins of others before them. He said in verse 4, "*The soul who sins will die.*"

While judgment will come for sins personally committed, the effect of sin is often passed on from one generation to the next. The social actions of a man will always affect others in that society. In America the fathers have eaten the sour grapes of atheism and now the children's teeth have been set on edge by drugs, declining education, and death in the schools.

The fathers had a taste of atheism when prayer and Bible reading were removed from the schools; an effort instigated by one woman. She was the "Eve" of our time -- in a place where she had no business being, and eating that which should have been left alone, enabling Satan to use her to fullest advantage.

The public schools became totally secular with the removal of any reference to the Christian God, creating a vacuum that Satan was all too willing to fill. Just as heat always flows from a hot object to a cooler one, morals tend to gravitate according to the surroundings. When godly influences are absent from a setting, the spiritual fires quickly die down, allowing the coldness of sin to become the prevailing wind -- an ill wind that is blowing through our schools and colleges today.

Since the liberal agenda has its roots in Satanic influence we should expect nothing but deception from those proposing the changes. Every desired turn on that devilish highway is presented with half-truths and depends on emotional appeal. In the matter of school prayer and Bible reading, it was based on the greatly misunderstood claim of separation of church and state and the foolish assumption that students' feelings might be hurt if it was allowed to continue.

It is no wonder that God said, *"Are My ways not right, O house of Israel? Is it not your ways that are not right?"* (Exe. 18:29) Replacing the name "Israel" with "America" makes the statement just as applicable.

Since atheism has been reigning in our schools, our children's health and welfare have become a major issue. When God was forced out of school, drugs came in, causing health, discipline, and learning problems. Some of those drugs are legal, recommended by counselors to better acclimate a student with supposed psychological problems, but usually ends in trading one problem for another.

Considering the great deal of time children spend in school, from pre-school to high school graduation, are we complying with God's commandment to *train up a child in the way he should go* (Proverbs 22:6), by way of atheistic teaching? Not likely.

Church and State

Unless the Lord builds the house, they labor in vain who build it; ... (Psalm 127:1) That's a simple statement, easily understood by anyone who believes the truth of God. No matter whose idea it was, or how much work is put into it by men and women, the success and longevity of a project is ultimately in the hands of God. It doesn't matter whether you are building a house, a city, a nation, or an institution; if God is not included, the laborers build in vain.

Until the 1960s God was included in the building of our education system. Clergy men were most always on hand for the dedication of a new school building to offer a prayer of thanksgiving and to request the Lord's blessing on the teachers and students. Each day's lessons were preceded by a short time of prayer and Bible reading, and the graduation ceremony always included the participation of a local pastor.

But, a funny thing happened on the way to the diploma. Somewhere along the line a few ungodly radicals with loud voices produced enough intimidation among our political representatives and judges to bring the issue of church and state to the foreground. Those people were allowed to twist the phrase, "separation of church and state," into something it never was, and the liberal media who claim to be honestly giving us an unbiased report on the news of the day, did nothing to stop that false claim.

The first amendment to the Constitution says, "Congress shall make no law respecting an establishment of religion, or prohibiting the free exercise thereof; or abridging the freedom of speech, or of the press, or the right of the people peaceably to assemble, and to petition the Government for a redress of grievances."

Well, anyone who has completed elementary school should be able to understand that the first part of the first amendment prohibits the federal government from passing a law that establishes a religion or names an existing one as the official religion of the state. That's what it says. No interpretation by any court is necessary. Show me the law passed by Congress that says Christianity is the official state religion. Congress never even attempted to pass such a law.

The second part of the passage on religion states that there shall be no "prohibiting the free exercise" of any religion. Show me the law passed by Congress that says Christians can't exercise their right to worship as they please. Congress would have to pass a law to support or prohibit religion, but it has never done that. Plain and simple, Congress cannot prohibit the people from exercising their religion in any place at any time. The Constitution prohibits such a law. Do you see now, how the "separation of church and state" has been turned upside down?

The major point in the loosely based argument for this separation is the government funding of public schools. Some people say that since the state must stay separated from the church, any aspect of religion must be removed from a government funded school so as not to be interpreted as government establishing a state religion. But just because the government provides funding for public schools does not mean it is supporting any religion taught or referred to there.

But if the liberals are correct in their interpretation, what about all the households that receive government welfare payments or unemployment or disability compensation? If government money is going into those homes, shouldn't all Bibles, crosses, and any other displays such as the Ten Commandments be removed? Shouldn't any prayer or Bible reading be prohibited? Should that family even be allowed to attend any church services while receiving a government dole?

The fact is, the Constitution does not prevent the government from merely giving money to any institution, religious or otherwise. For example, if each congressional budget included a donation to the Methodist Church without any stipulations pertaining to power or authority of that religious group, it would not be unconstitutional. As long as the Church received no endorsement, was not granted any special powers, or was not limited in its actions, and as long as Congress passed no law of establishment, there would be no violation.

It doesn't matter how much money Congress gives to public schools. The Constitution states that Congress cannot pass a law that establishes a religion, and since Congress can never pass such a law, any religious activity in a public school that is receiving federal money will never be unconstitutional.

If government is to be separated from all religion why are any religious men and women allowed to run for office? Shouldn't there be a sign at all political party headquarters saying no Christians need apply? Shouldn't State and Federal governments be composed of atheists only, in order to present a true separation of church and state?

If separation of church and state is as the liberals see it, how is it that a professing Christian man, in the person of George W. Bush, came to be President? Could that be the underlying reason why he has been so hated by the liberals? Never mind the war in Iraq; go back to the 2000 campaign when Bush was asked whom he most admired and his answer was, "Christ." That is the root cause of the liberal hatred for that man. Jesus called such spiteful people hypocrites and blind guides.

The irony of this whole issue is that Congress has actually done nothing one way or the other concerning the separation of church and state. It has never violated the Constitution by attempting to pass a law that established a particular religion as the religion of the State, and it has never prevented the people from exercising their constitutional rights on that matter. The interference has come from the courts.

It's another smoke and mirrors tactic. Satan has used such strategy often, down through the ages, and his instruments, the ungodly liberals, have used it to perfection. The politicians have taken no action either way, but rest in the popular belief (falsely) that Congress is bound by the constitutional separation of church and state.

That's a fact that a lot of people don't understand, which explains why the liberal interpretation of separation of church and state has prevailed. Congress has shirked its duties by allowing the courts to "write law" through their rulings, thereby escaping the wrath of voters at election time. Anytime a Congressman is asked about the wraps on religion, he merely spouts the separation of church and state line, implying there is nothing he can do. The Supreme Court gods have spoken.

Through their inaction, the members of Congress are guilty of allowing our freedom of worship to be usurped by the ACLU lawyers and the men and women in black robes. It's just one of many reasons why Congress should be turned out of office.

School Prayer

Another part of the flawed liberal argument is of the rights of the students to not have a religion forced upon them. There's another irony. The American Revolution was conducted because of limited rights, but in our time we are overburdened with "rights." It seems that everybody has the right to everything, to the point where now we have the freedom of nothing. Emotions set the standards of the day. How someone feels about something determines how the rest of us are to correspondingly act. The liberals have long complained that conservatives are trying to legislate morality while the liberal courts have steadily ruled in favor of moral change, mostly to the detriment of our moral standards.

It is said that too many children were forced to participate in school prayer and Bible reading, causing much stress and embarrassment for them. Does anyone know of any child who came home from school complaining of that activity? When we hear of the lawsuits brought by protective parents, investigation usually shows that the parent is an atheist or member of some radical group, or both. It isn't the child's wishes to be free of exposure to God; it's the wishes of the parents, using the child as a means of pushing their agenda.

Another objection to prayer and Bible reading is over the different religions of children in the public schools. It is said that it's not fair to Jewish, Muslim, Hindu, etc., to have to sit through Christian indoctrination, but if the matter is of great importance to such a family, they have the option to send their children to a school that promotes their religious faith.

I sat through twelve years of prayer and Bible reading in a public school and not once felt intimidated to make any profession of faith or join any church. Neither did I hear any of my classmates complain of such treatment. Those few minutes each morning when the teacher read a few verses of scripture and led us in the Lord's Prayer was nothing more than acknowledgment of the sovereignty of God and a reminder of how we should live to be good citizens. Only an atheist or an anti-American would protest. The question is, why has such a small minority been allowed to force their beliefs on the majority? This is not something that should be happening and it is not an issue that we can do nothing about.

But remember, the war is primarily between Jesus and Satan, therefore the main assault is against Christianity. If it was not the Christian Bible that was being read from, and not the Lord's Prayer that was being recited, the issue would not exist. Indeed, in some public schools there are classes that introduce children to religions other than Christianity, and where are the "separatists" then? If the children are being taught what is in the Koran, is the government not sponsoring that religion? It would seem so according to the liberal interpretation of separation of church and state.

Woe to the rebellious children, declares the Lord, who execute a plan, but not Mine, and make an alliance, but not of My Spirit, in order to add sin to sin; (Isaiah 30:1)

It was the intervention of God that established this great country and the same hand that enabled it to exist through revolutionary, civil, and world war. Though we often went about things the wrong way, there was still an overriding desire to live according to the principles found in the Christian Bible. The people of this land gave glory to God in all of its institutions, with His presence being noted in our government, on our money, and at any public event. During times of crisis we were encouraged by our leaders to pray to this God for deliverance. That's how it was until the 1960s.

Since that time our Christian beliefs have been under attack with some of our religious freedom already suppressed. The rebellion started by the liberals in the 1960s brought about a new plan for the education of our children and it definitely was not God's plan. The people who have taken control of our education system have made an alliance with the devil and we are seeing the activity of Satan in our public schools by way of drugs, declining learning, and death.

In Luke 18:15-16 there's an account of people bringing their children to Jesus for a blessing but His disciples decided that it was too much of an imposition and began turning them away. Jesus' response was, *"Permit the children to come to Me, and do not hinder them, for the kingdom of God belongs to such as these."* Jesus is now sitting at the right hand of God. What do you think might Their response be to elimination of prayer and Bible reading in the schools?

Secularism

For not knowing about God's righteousness, and seeking to establish their own, they did not subject themselves to the righteousness of God. (Romans 10:3)

A person who is ungodly is one who is not in a right spiritual relationship with God because of rejection of Jesus Christ as the only way to God. Ungodly actions are those which are contrary to the principles of God's Word and produce a result that is undesirable in God's sight, as based on His word, the Bible.

Uninformed Christians may find themselves supporting an ungodly agenda because they have failed to compare the liberal agenda with God's word and have been taken in by the wonderful sounding clichés. The liberal activists sound well-intentioned and phrase their terms to give the appearance of having everyone's interest at heart, including the elderly, the sick and diseased, the starving and homeless, and especially the children. How can anyone be against helping the unfortunate and innocent?

They appeal to your emotions, trying to instill a sense of guilt. The liberal media who publicize those good intentions never give us an update on how badly those programs fail, how much they cost and how many lives were harmed, rather than helped.

The ungodly liberals are so because they don't know about God's righteousness and therefore are not subjecting themselves to it. They don't want to know it, either.

Professing to be wise, they became fools, (Rom.1:22) and, *For they exchanged the truth of God for a lie, and worshiped and served the creature rather than the Creator, ...* (Rom. 1:25) so, *... God gave them over to a depraved mind, to do those things which are not proper,* (Rom. 1:28)

The secular world is a world without God that is presently tolerating the Christians. There will come a time when that tolerance will be extended to every religious and racial group except the Christians. Christ said that if they persecuted Him, we could expect the same treatment.

We are presently controlled by the thought process of fools who profess to be wise. They act like a child who has grown up and doesn't need the security blanket of religion anymore. They will believe any new teaching on life, death, origins, endings, and morality, while rejecting the truth of God. More attention is given to the earth and its creatures than the God who created them. The more adamant people become about such things, the more likely it is that God will reject them.

See to it that no one takes you captive through philosophy and empty deception, according to the tradition of men, according to the elementary principles of the world, rather than according to Christ. (Colossians 2:8)

Stalin in Russia, Hitler in Germany, and Hussein in Iraq did no greater work for Satan in the twentieth century than the liberal college professors of America. Our institutions of higher learning have served as a cradle for the nourishment and growth of the ungodly liberal agenda. They are the enemy who has planted the tares among the wheat, filling the minds of our bright young people with godless philosophy and deception.

It is bad enough to be an unbeliever, but the one who leads others into that error will receive the greater condemnation. In Matthew 18:6, Jesus said, *"but whoever causes one of these little ones who believe in Me to stumble, it is better for him that a heavy millstone be hung around his neck, and that he be drowned in the depth of the sea."*

Many parents have wondered what happened to their previously faithful children after returning from college, spouting the liberal philosophy and praising the tradition of men rather than faithfulness to Christ. Sometimes this occurs while the student is still in high school after sitting through a class taught by one who has had the liberal college brainwashing, or one who used to be a college professor. Some teachers and professors spend their time on political science rather than the subject they are supposed to be teaching.

The "elementary principles of the world" mean the same thing as "conventional wisdom," but it is well to remember that conventional wisdom is always on a different road than God. If you want to know how God *doesn't* do things, look at conventional wisdom or the tradition of men. His ways are not our ways.

And do not be conformed to this world, but be transformed by the renewing of your mind, that you may prove what the will of God is, that which is good and acceptable and perfect. (Romans 12:2)

Since God is at enmity with the world His natural desire is for us to *not* be conformed to the world. As the apostle Paul said, *"Be imitators of me, just as I also am of Christ."* (I Corinthians 11:1) God saved us … *according to His mercy, by the washing of regeneration and renewing by the Holy Spirit.* (Titus 3:5)

When we were born again, we were given a new nature which is not something to be taken lightly. Through the grace of God, we were washed and made new by the Holy Spirit. As a result of that wondrous work of God, we now have the ability to renew our minds, which takes awhile, but will result in a definite transformation of our character, and that's what God wants to see.

Of course, as that transformation takes place, we will also be at enmity with the world and should not be surprised by ridicule, condemnation, castigation, and persecution from the unbelievers of the world. Therefore, Christians should understand that there will be no such godly transformation of their children in public school or college.

The administrators of those places have already made that clear through their adherence to the separation of church and state myth.

The responsibility of the child's transformation lies with the parents. Christian education occurs only in the local church through effective preaching, Sunday school, and other means such as youth ministries and vacation Bible schools during summer. But the foundation is laid at home. Children need to be taught the word of God at the earliest age and their faith nurtured through family Bible study and prayer time. A faithful example by the parents is of tremendous value to the child.

With such a strong foundation laid and continuing maintenance of faith, the child is much less likely to become conformed to the atheistic teaching of the public schools. It is such a sad thing when parents place full reliance on the school for their child's education and neglect completely the Christian training that is so needed. Truly, a double error with grave consequences.

Being transformed by the renewing of your mind proves the will of God and brings about that which is good, acceptable, and perfect. God wants only good for us and takes great pleasure in giving good things to us. Our transformation results in a life that is acceptable in God's sight and a life that displays the perfection of God.

Wouldn't you think that a public school would strive to be a place where that which is good and acceptable and perfect is taught? It used to be, but during the last half of the twentieth century the public schools have given themselves over to vain philosophy and empty deception, promoting self, (which God has always condemned), by way of self esteem, tolerance, and sensitivity. Is it a coincidence that since public schools tossed out good, acceptable, and perfect in favor of self esteem, tolerance, and sensitivity, the problems of our schools have reached the point of crisis?

Here's another consideration. The method of teaching in the public schools of the first half of the twentieth century turned out generations who won a world war and produced a technology unmatched by any people in any time. Perhaps we should have paid more attention to that old adage, "if it ain't broke, don't fix it."

... but when they measure themselves by themselves, and compare themselves with themselves, they are without understanding. (II Corinthians 10:12) Paul was speaking of people who rejected the truth of his letters

and were overly confident of their own abilities. Such are the liberals of our day.

To the liberal mind, it doesn't matter how many times in history their idea has been tried and failed; what matters is their intentions. Their own failures are ignored or blamed on another part of society, usually a conservative faction.

Curriculum

The apostle Paul gave Timothy some very good advice as he urged him to remain at Ephesus and "*... instruct certain men not to teach strange doctrines, nor to pay attention to myths and endless genealogies, which give rise to mere speculation rather than furthering the administration of God which is by faith."* (I Timothy 1:3-4)

The reason for this advice was *"For some men, straying from these things, have turned aside to fruitless discussion, wanting to be teachers of the Law, even though they do not understand either what they are saying or the matters about which they make confident assertions.* (I Timothy 1:6-7)

The matters of which Paul was speaking concerned the preaching of the gospel which was a new covenant in Christ. Some men were not presenting this gospel in its purest form, but were adding alien doctrines and including other aspects as fact, but really was nothing more than speculation. They spent too much time talking about unimportant things, failing to enlighten anyone, mainly because they were getting into areas in which they had no knowledge. Our school board members would do well to advise the faculty in the same manner.

The time of this country's greatest expansion that elevated America to the status of the leading nation of the world was also the time when God was acknowledged as the one who provided the means for such an achievement. Throughout history, whenever a nation raised to that position rejected the teachings of God, the demise of that nation soon followed. America began its turn away from the Creator in the 1960s and now the serious problems are developing faster than we can solve them.

As if removing prayer and Bible reading were not enough, the textbooks present the myth of evolution as though it is scientific fact when it is nothing more than speculation. Charles Darwin's treatise on the origin of species was correctly labeled as a *theory* but in today's institutions of learning it is never presented as a theory only. Geologists and anthropologists have been looking at rocks and bones and making educated guesses. Since evolutionists claim that the process occurred over millions of years there is no way evolution can be scientifically demonstrated or observed. There is not enough time.

Textbooks of deception have gained entrance to the schools at the same time the greatest textbook of all time, the Bible, has been banned. The great misunderstanding is that the Bible is not only a spiritual, religious book, but one of scientific value that gives much insight into the mysteries of the earth and universe as a whole.

Here we see another example of how a natural vacuum cannot exist in God's eternal purpose. The truth of God was evicted from the schools and the deception of Satan came flowing in. We should be very careful about excluding God from anything.

Paul asked an appropriate question of the people of Galatia. *"You were running well; who hindered you from obeying the truth? This persuasion did not come from Him who calls you."* (Galatians 5:7-8) Does anyone with even the slightest faith in God actually believe that He is indifferent to our eliminating His presence from our schools? We have a complete book that says God is not indifferent to such things. How is it that the Christians of America have so meekly accepted that turn of events?

Jesus certainly did speak well when He described His people as sheep. If we know our Shepherd's voice, why don't we turn out of office the ones who cater to the Satanic minority that have brought myths, speculation, and fruitless discussion into our schools? During national elections, too many Christians fall for the liberal feel-good message and the lie that they only have our best interests at heart. Too many Christians are looking to the government for provision when they should be looking to God. To whom are you giving glory if you put your trust in government and vote for the person whose political party pushes the ungodly agenda?

Following his question, Paul gives a warning. *"A little leaven leavens the whole lump of dough."* (Gal. 5:9) Yes, if you put a little yeast in a mixture of dough, knead it awhile, then let it sit, that small amount of yeast will affect the whole lump, making it bigger than it was.

The ungodly instruction went from teaching evolution to teaching kids about sex in a way that allowed them to be sexually active before they had the maturity to understand it, or the wisdom of sex only within a marriage. Then they were taught that the homosexual lifestyle was an acceptable family lifestyle, providing everything found in a normal family of male/female parents.

The perversion has progressed to the point where the national news presented a case of a panel of "experts" telling kids in a certain school they would be taught how to enjoy sex with opposite or same-sex partners and how to safely use illegal drugs. The progression of evil in our schools will not stop until there is genuine repentance.

My people are destroyed for lack of knowledge. Because you have rejected knowledge, I also will reject you from being My priest. Since you have forgotten the law of your God, I also will forget your children. (Hosea 4:6)

The prophet Hosea was speaking to the northern kingdom of Israel around 750 B.C., but his message sheds much light on school problems 2700 years later. Educators are keepers of the knowledge of the world but they are devoid of the knowledge of God. That's what Hosea is talking about. A lack of knowledge of God and His ways brings poverty and destruction. It isn't as though the people in charge of our education system never heard of or have no means of acquiring that knowledge; they had it and rejected it.

Israel was to be a priestly nation to the world but God said He would remove them from that distinction. God raised up the United States as a repository for His word and as a stabilizing force for the reestablishment of Israel in the Middle East. Through most of our history we have not only kept that faith and knowledge but have done more for, and given more to, other nations of the world than any other nation in history.

America has excelled in missionary work and the printing and distribution of Bibles in most languages of the world. Many educational religious institutions still perform that work but the secular public school has dropped the ball. The educators of our children have turned them away from God and every time there is a school shooting or some other disaster or outrage, we ask why, and start looking for the root causes. The root cause is they have forgotten the law of our God, and He has "forgotten" our children. A minimum of common sense should make the connection.

Money

Men prepare a meal for enjoyment, and wine makes life merry, and money is the answer to everything. (Ecclesiastes 10:19)

It all started with Sputnik. That little basketball-sized satellite that Russia put into orbit in October of 1957. Even though that's all the Soviets were capable of, (the satellite had no scientific capabilities – just beeped its way around the world), a great panic arose over the supposed science-education gap between us and the Russians. We needed smarter kids and we needed them now! The best money could buy!

That was the first manufactured liberal crisis of our modern age, but education wasn't the problem at all. Our space technology easily outstripped the Soviets; we just took a little more time, being more careful, and developed a more worth-while venture. Just twelve years later we landed men on the moon, something the Soviets were never able to accomplish.

If education was the determining factor in the space race, then we have to assume the people working on that program were better educated in the Russian schools of the 1930s and 1940s than their American counterparts. Conditions were very harsh in Russia at that time, so, if that environment produced better educated students, why have we spent billions on new, comfortable schools and methods where students would no longer feel any pressure and learn at their own pace, with no child being left behind? Shouldn't we have preferred more Spartan schools with a stricter learning environment as the Russians had?

Let's take a realistic look at our side of it. In 1957 we decide we need a better system of education, but how long will it take to make all the changes that will produce a much better system? The debate, legislation and funding usually takes a year or so to get going, and how many years will it take to decide on a new course of study and produce the updated textbooks?

How much time is involved in the merging of school districts, acquiring land to build new schools, and the actual building of those schools? My own school district announced in my senior year of '58-'59 that it would merge with another district and build a new school. That new school received its first students in the fall of 1961, a few months after we sent the first American into space on a sub-orbital flight.

The first graduating class that spent all twelve years in the new system (which merged into a bigger district in 1966) with its new methods like the "new math," was the class of 1973, four years after we landed men on the moon. Not one of those NASA scientists learned their trade in the new American schools of the sixties. So, the question is, how did we suddenly become smarter than the Russians? The answer is, we always were.

It was the men and women of science (with the help of a few German rocket scientists) who were working on the space mission for years. As a matter of fact, it was our technology that made it possible to build a missile defense system (which we only threatened to build) that brought about the collapse of the Soviet Union. The point is, there was no education crisis. It was an opportunity for the liberals to seize control of a most important system, an outstanding coup on their part, that enabled them to begin a systematic indoctrination of our children through an ungodly learning process.

But costly new buildings and a deceptive curriculum wasn't enough. Teachers unions were formed to solidify their power and the Department of Education was established in 1979 to provide total control. Money was the answer to our supposed education problems but after fifty years of change, how did things turn out? How is our new house of education standing up?

Ecclesiastes 10:18 says it best. *"Through indolence the rafters sag, and through slackness the house leaks."* The indolence of the school administrators in allowing God to be kicked out of school, and the willingness of many teachers in complying with the liberal mantra of maintaining the importance of self-esteem and tolerance, rather than focusing on the fundamentals, has not raised the grades of school children or produced a better educated graduating class. If it has, why do we still keep hearing from the news media that American kids are lagging behind the students of other countries?

The American children of the first half of the twentieth century were receiving a better education for less cost than those of the second half of that century. Oh, it was a much simpler time, you say; there wasn't as much to learn. Yes, it was a simpler time, but the methods of that time nurtured the intellect of that earlier group that produced the technology of the later time.

What are the fruits of the latter group? Drug and discipline problems, teen pregnancies, school dropouts, illiterate graduates, juvenile crime, etc. *"Why do you spend money for what is not bread, and your wages for what does not satisfy?"* (Isaiah 55:2) Yes, why do we keep pouring money into such an educational system? And why aren't the liberal failed programs ever investigated?

Every major issue of the liberal agenda is ungodly, therefore, nothing but deception. Not one of their issues is a crisis. Education wasn't in a crisis mode until the liberals got control of it. Education is a crisis in 2010, but it wasn't a crisis in 1957 when the activists started their push.

Whatever the issue, it goes the same way. It doesn't matter whether it is global warming, global cooling, racism, immigration, the economy, starving and homeless people in America, obesity, or whatever. A few baseless "facts" are thrown up, a few "victims" are trotted out, and suddenly we have a crisis; one that only the liberal Democratic politicians can solve. The news media love a crisis – it makes for great headlines and TV ratings.

Microphones and cameras are shoved into the faces of common people as they are asked if they want clean air and water, well-fed children, homes and jobs for everybody, TVs, two cars, and a chicken in every pot. And who would say no to any of that? The liberals then build their case and their movement gains momentum as "the American people" want all these things. Satan is still using the same method of deception that worked for him in the Garden of Eden with Eve, and the American people are still fooled every time a national election rolls around.

Education is an ungodly liberal issue because it rejects God, teaches the children an ungodly way, and usurps the authority of parents over their children. The amount of money required to support the public schools is obscene; forcing some of the citizenry to pay an unreasonable amount.

Solution

What is the solution? We should do what our purpose on earth is – give glory to God. Acknowledge the existence of a sovereign God and His participation in the affairs of men at the beginning of every school day by reading a passage of God's word to the class. If a teacher claims to be an atheist, then let that teacher find a position in a school of atheism, or another line of work. Why should we expose our children to the poison of atheism?

If a student is offended by the reading, let him or her stand outside the classroom for that brief period, or let their parents take full responsibility for their education if the Christian faith is not compatible with their belief. This country was founded on Christian principles, no matter what the ungodly say. It was a country that gave glory to the God of Christianity for 175 years. No person of any other religious belief has the right to restrict the Christian religion in America any more than a Christian has the right to call for a restriction on Islam in Saudi Arabia, or on Hinduism in India. People of other faiths may live peaceably in America but they have no business objecting to our Christian religion. In most Islamic and Hinduistic countries, a person who converts to Christianity is not tolerated at all. Such a one is usually persecuted severely. Why do we subject Christianity to the demands of an ungodly religion? By doing so, we're saying that Christianity is not the only Way. Was Jesus ever willing to defer to the unbelievers of His time? Did He ever compromise and tone down His message? Did He not say, "*I am the way, and the truth, and the life; no one comes to the Father, but through Me.*" (John 14:6) Why are we so willing to make that compromise?

All we need are citizens, politicians, and judges who have the courage and conviction to stand up for the truth of Christ. Are there enough of such people left in the land of America? Pray that it is so.

Chapter Seven

GOVERNMENT

Encourages Trust in Human Institutions

Trust

God's preference of government on earth is a Theocracy. *For the Lord Most High is to be feared, a great King over all the earth.* (Psalm 47:2)

In the fifteenth century B.C., God had just brought into existence a new nation – Israel. Since God knew everything and Israel knew next to nothing, it was His intention to rule over the nation and provide the people with a set of civil and moral laws to live by. The system would be a Theocracy; one in which God would rule through priests and judges. God would establish them in a land of abundance, meeting all their needs and protecting them from the surrounding heathen nations. All the people had to do was acknowledge God as sovereign and be obedient to all of His commandments. *It is better to take refuge in the Lord than to trust in princes.* (Psalm 118:9)

That system of government lasted about 400 years with the Israelites continually breaking God's laws and coming up short, experiencing much tribulation along the way because of their disobedience. Eventually they asked for a king, to be more like the other nations, so God granted their request but warned of the consequences.

That's how it started and that's how it will end -- as a Theocracy with Jesus Christ being here in person, ruling over all nations. In between those times some form of government is necessary to have law and order among the peoples of the world.

And in the generations gone by He permitted all the nations to go their own ways; (Acts 14:16) The human race would have nothing to do with a Theocracy. All the heathen nations had a king, with Israel following suit at the coronation of King Saul.

Any particular form of government is what the people choose or what they allow to be in place because of indifference or fear. It can be a monarchy with a king, such as ancient Israel; a parliamentary form of government as in England; or a representative system (democracy) as in the United States. In some countries a communist or socialist government rules, and in most Muslim countries the government is heavily influenced by their religious beliefs. There are countries where people are ruled by a political or military dictator – benevolent or otherwise.

The point is, all governments are permitted by God in bringing about His eternal purpose. A government may serve as a blessing to His people or as a curse upon the wicked. God has given us much instruction in His written word about how a government should operate and how the people should respond.

In America God prepared a refuge for many of His persecuted people of the Old World. In spite of what the ungodly liberals of today say about religion, many of the people who settled this land believed in God and the Savior Jesus Christ. Only the hand of God can account for the founding, preservation, and technical/industrial development of the United States.

America was never a 100% Christian nation, totally following the word of God, as there is much historical evidence to the contrary. We didn't always do what was right and we didn't always treat certain citizens as brothers and sisters in the Lord. But even though our ancestors often came up short (as did the Israelites) they still had a high sense of morality and responsibility which guided their actions. They still believed that God was sovereign, a sovereign Being who forces everyone into a future accountability.

This belief enabled them to gradually overcome the ways of the Old World culture, eliminating the class systems between royalty and peasantry, ending slavery and allowing people to live in a more dignified manner. Most importantly, freedom to worship in the Christian religion prevailed and great importance was placed on the value of proper education.

America became the greatest carrier of good news, the Gospel, taking it to every accessible nation. We also became the most generous and helpful country that ever existed on earth, spreading our wealth and ingenuity around the world. People from every land have always wanted to come to America. Even though the liberal media often describe us as a mean-spirited, selfish country, we currently have a critical immigration problem as foreigners are still trying to get into the USA by any means possible.

Around the middle of the twentieth century our values and beliefs began to change, due largely to the actions and in some cases, inaction, of our government. The morality of the Bible began to be shoved aside and the Christian religion came to be known as one of suppression. During the age of "civil rights" it became an easy thing to throw off the heavy yoke of religion, freeing people to do their own thing and worship whatever they chose to believe in.

In recent times the posting of the Ten Commandments on government property, local, state, or federal, has become a big issue; one that has arisen over the distorted claim of separation of church and state. We need only to look at the first of those Ten Commandments to see why. *You shall have no other gods before Me.* (Exodus 20:3)

Our government has diminished the sovereignty of God, taking upon itself the full responsibility of its citizens' lives. Rather than merely providing for our national security against foreign powers as it was intended to do, government has taken on the role of provider and sustainer of the staples of life, telling us that it is our only source of everything. *Do not trust in princes, in mortal man, in whom there is no salvation.* (Psalm 146:3)

Is it any wonder that our politicians don't want to see the Commandments posted in the halls and chambers of government buildings? The very first of those Commandments places government in a secondary position when it comes to ruling over people's lives, a position where no politician or bureaucrat ever wants to be.

God does not look favorably upon a people who empower their government to be their sole provider. Many of the condemnations listed in the Bible against the Israelites apply to us because we are guilty of the same crimes against God. His laws of morality and sovereignty apply to all the people of the world, not just ancient Israel.

Thus says the Lord, "Cursed is the man who trusts in mankind and makes flesh his strength, and whose heart turns away from the Lord.' (Jeremiah 17:5)

In making a distinction between the godly and ungodly, Psalm 68:6 says, *God makes a home for the lonely; He leads out the prisoners into prosperity, only the rebellious dwell in a parched land.*

Those who rebel against God and do not believe His word are destined to live without His blessing. In the aftermath of the great flood, certain descendants of Noah moved into Africa and toward the far east, not taking the God of their ancestors with them, resulting in a worship of false gods and supernatural beliefs. The nations that grew from those tribes have continually experienced the ravages of natural disaster in the form of earthquake, flood, drought, disease and famine, more so than other parts of the world.

There was no form of reliable government among those nations until established by the European colonists. While most of the uncolonized countries remained in a somewhat primitive state, steeped in the supernatural, the colonies began to realize a gradual benefit. True, the colonists were more interested in the material wealth to be gained from those countries rather than serving as graceful benefactors, but in that process established law and order and generally raised the standard of living for the native peoples.

However, after the colonies were granted independence during the twentieth century it became apparent that citizens with no experience in running a democratic form of government had great difficulty in the workings of such an undertaking, reverting back to tribalism. That system resulted in continual warfare among the strongmen with no care for the welfare of the general population, producing mass killings and many displaced persons. The additional problems of disease, famine, and drought were greatly multiplied as there was no one in a leadership role possessing the knowledge to combat those apocalyptic horsemen. And, in the case of some, South Africa for example, while the citizens have retained the democratic government, its extreme liberal policies have allowed the nation to begin sinking back into poverty.

See, I have set before you today life and prosperity, and death and adversity; (Deut. 30:15) Moses spoke those words of God to the Israelites as they prepared to enter the promised land. It was a fork in the road, marked by obedience to God and His laws. An acceptance of His command to honor and obey brought life and prosperity; a rejection brought death and adversity.

It is easy to see which nations chose life, carrying the word of God with them and eventually accepting the gospel of Christ. It is the major difference between the civilized and the uncivilized. We do well in charitable giving to the poor countries of the world but without the gospel and a majority of those citizens trusting in God, and faithful leaders, it is unlikely that the woeful conditions of many countries around the world will ever be changed. We just keep treating the symptoms.

Choose wise and discerning and experienced men from your tribes, and I will appoint them as your heads. (Deut. 1:13)

Purpose

So now we come to the purpose of government. Being the Book of Life, the Bible gives detailed instruction on everything, including government. The best passage on the subject can be found in Romans 13:1-5.

Let every person be in subjection to the governing authorities. For there is no authority except from God, and those which exist are established by God. (2) Therefore he who resists authority has opposed the ordinance of God; and they who have opposed will receive condemnation upon themselves. (3) For rulers are not a cause of fear for good behavior, but for evil. Do you want to have no fear of authority? Do what is good, and you will have praise from the same; (4) for it is a minister of God to you for good. But if you do what is evil, be afraid; for it does not bear the sword for nothing; for it is a minister of God, an avenger who brings wrath upon the one who practices evil. (5) Wherefore it is necessary to be in subjection, not only because of wrath, but also for conscience' sake.

The first thing that needs to be understood about this passage is that it states the way things *should* be; not how they are. If godly people are living under the direction of godly leaders there will be no cause for fear or rebellion. The problem arises when ungodliness creeps in among the people and becomes pervasive in legislative bodies and bureaucracies. The self-serving workings of our current state and federal governing systems are a natural result.

The Bible tells us that all governing authorities, good or bad, exist because of the allowance of God. The natural question to that statement is, "Then, if God is good, why does He allow bad governments to exist?" The answer is, because God is just, and because of the disobedience of people. In some cases, God will not only allow a bad government to be in power, but will actually raise one up as a chastisement upon His people, or to bring about His wrath upon the ungodly.

God gives the people of any nation the kind of government they deserve. If we have an immoral, oppressive government, maybe we need to look within ourselves to ascertain our relationship with God.

Verse two of that passage in Romans, chapter 13, causes an interesting question. It says that if we resist authority, we are opposing the ordinance of God. Okay, but then, what about revolution against an oppressive authority to gain independence, such as the American Revolution? Was that cause against the ordinance of God?

The key to understanding is remembering that all authority is established by God who works through the means of men, using them as His instruments for blessing or wrath. God doesn't always cause certain people, or whole groups of people, to die suddenly from a plague when He no longer wants them on this earth. They die, or are taken out of the picture in other ways because of their actions or the actions of other men under the direction of God. He will use both good and evil persons to bring about change, depending upon the circumstances, and sometimes He will use His control of the environment to eradicate evil persons and to bring about a sudden change of ways.

Whatever the Lord pleases, He does, in heaven and in earth, in the seas and in all deeps. (Psalm 135:6) In the case of revolution, it will occur when it is decreed by God. The timing will be right and the method will be right. It doesn't matter what the reasons are in the minds of the rebels; if God wants drastic change at that time, then change will happen. If no divine guarantee is given, revolution may still take place but it will be in vain. Two examples are the American Revolution and our Civil War.

It is now evident that in 1776 God desired to bring forth on this continent a new nation, conceived in liberty and dedicated to the proposition that all men are created equal. (Thanks to Abraham Lincoln for that beautiful statement of truth.) God raised up men of high moral capacity who rebelled against the self-serving authority of King George. It didn't matter that the royal oppression was not near as great as that from our government today; God wanted revolution and revolution occurred.

The historical evidence shows that the colonists were undermanned, underarmed, and underfed, and shouldn't have won that war according to conventional wisdom, but, no matter; *Through God we shall do valiantly, and it is He who will tread down our adversaries.* (Psalm 60:12)

The colonists' mindset was based on Biblical principles. They believed the scriptures, they believed in prayer, they believed in the providence of God, and they weren't afraid to state those beliefs and call upon others to be in like manner. Think of what happens to candidates who speak that way in a Presidential campaign in our time.

In the case of the Civil War, I'm sure the confederates thought they were embarking on a just cause of States' rights and were imploring God to deliver them from the oppression of the Federal government, but apparently it was not part of God's plan to have a divided America from that time forward. Another consideration is that God may have been "paying" the Southerners for their own oppression of the blacks in slavery. At any rate, God did not deliver the victory to the rebels in that case.

God gives us further instruction on how to conduct ourselves concerning the government in I Peter 2:13-17. *Submit yourselves for the Lord's sake to every human institution, whether to a king as the one in authority, (14) or to governors as sent by him for the punishment of evildoers and the praise of those who do right. (15) For such is the will of God that by doing right you may silence the ignorance of foolish men. (16) Act as free men, and do not use your freedom as a covering for evil, but use it as bond slaves of God. (17) Honor all men; love the brotherhood, fear God, honor the king.*

We are to be in submission to all the laws of Congress and all the regulations of the bureaucracies. If such laws and regulations are unbearable we have the privilege of voting more reasonable men and women into office to relieve the burden. The effect of legislation upon the population, or certain members of it, is an accurate reflection of the hearts and minds of those who pass such legislation. More attention should be paid to what legislators do, than what they say. More legislators should be held accountable for the harmful bills they have pushed through the state and federal houses. Such legislation is trumpeted as help to a group of victimized people but is designed to merely further their political careers by getting the votes of those people.

While it is true that a heavy handed government causes much hardship on many people, we are encouraged to do right and be honest in all our affairs. *Remind them to be subject to rulers, to authorities, to be obedient, to be ready for every good deed,* (Titus 3:1)

Rather than taking steps to subvert our government, we should be electing upright people who are willing to oversee the affairs of state for a few years without making a career of it. The lifetime politicians are the ones that produce the graft and corruption. They campaign on their experience, but it is experience in taking more of our freedom and money to continue their lavish way of life as career politicians. When that experience shows up in our political servants, it is time to bring them back home to continue in their private professions.

We are to treat all men honorably and with love. We are to fear God and honor the one whom He has chosen to be our ruler for the time being. *First of all, then, I urge that entreaties and prayers, petitions and thanksgivings, be made on behalf of all men, (2) for kings and all who are in authority, in order that we may lead a tranquil and quiet life in all godliness and dignity.* (I Timothy 2:1-2)

Deceit

The key to perpetuating an ungodly government is deceit. As long as the perpetrators can mask their actions and get their constituents to believe every word, the truth remains hidden. Much help is received in that endeavor from the liberal media who feed the public misleading statistics and keep repeating the worn out clichés that pit the different income classes against one another. That tactic also works well in stirring the pot of race relations, immigration, and foreign policy.

God knows such people very well and has described them to perfection, as He does in all things. Read the following collection of verses that sound as though they could all have come from the same book and chapter, then we'll take a closer look at each one with commentary and identification.

Your rulers are rebels, and companions of thieves; everyone loves a bribe, and chases after rewards. Woe to those who call evil good, and good evil; who substitute darkness for light and light for darkness; who substitute bitter for sweet, and sweet for bitter! For where jealousy and selfish ambition exist, there is disorder and every evil thing. Her leaders pronounce judgment for a bribe, her priests instruct for a price, and her prophets divine for money. Yet they lean on the Lord saying, "Is not the Lord in our midst? Calamity will not come upon us." Holding to a form of godliness, although they have denied its power. And they have healed the brokenness of My people superficially, saying, 'peace, peace,' but there is no peace. For even your brothers and the household of your father, even they have dealt treacherously with you, even they have cried aloud after you. Do not believe them, although they may say nice things to you. Concerning evil, both hands do it well. The prince asks, also the judge, for a bribe, and a great man speaks the desire of his soul; so they weave it together. Woe to the rebellious children, declares the Lord, who execute a plan, but not Mine, and make an alliance, but not of My Spirit, in order to add sin to sin; The prophets prophesy falsely, and the priests rule on their own authority; and My people love it so! But what will you do at the end of it?

Quite an amazing passage, isn't it? Substitute president, senator, congressman, governor, mayor, commissioner, councilman, or supervisor, for the titles listed in those verses and they ring just as true. So now, let's take a closer look at each verse and allow a stronger light to reveal

God's opinion of men and women who get caught up in the trappings of ungodly political pursuit.

That first verse, *"Your rulers are rebels, and companions of thieves; everyone loves a bribe, and chases after rewards."* (Isaiah 1:23), should be the leading statement at the beginning of every major network news show every day and the front page headline of every newspaper. Those networks and newspapers that take pride in presenting the "truth" could truly feel good about themselves, and perhaps, shame those thieving politicians to turn over a new leaf.

Every new candidate is looked upon with hope that he or she will finally be the one to make an honest difference and that we can rely on them to always have the best interest of our country at heart. And, quite often we elect a truly honest person with good intentions, but when they get to the State House or Capitol building in Washington, D.C., they soon find that to get along they have to go along. It is difficult to resist temptation when you live in the house of the tempter.

After breathing deeply of the political atmosphere, the best interests of the country in general and the constituents in particular seem like stale air as the new legislator becomes one of the gang and whose main concern is now the next election. Their own income and welfare come first.

They take an inappropriate share of our money and waste it on pork barrel projects that benefit few, even transferring our Social Security Fund money into the general treasury so it could be used as they desired. They act as though they are entitled to our money to do with as they wish and take no responsibility for wasting it, becoming indignant when asked to make an accounting and blaming the members of the other political party.

Woe to those who call evil good, and good evil; who substitute darkness for light and light for darkness; who substitute bitter for sweet, and sweet for bitter! (Isaiah 5:20)

The elected servants experience a new outlook. Right and wrong become subject to desires. They agree with the liberal position of irresponsibility, assigning no blame or shame to wrong-doing but assign entitlement to anyone who may vote to reelect them. Their public relations people put a positive spin on their evil deeds claiming the alleged wrong is really right and as soon as the voters accept it, they will be much better off.

For where jealousy and selfish ambition exist, there is disorder and every evil thing. (James 3:16) Perhaps career politicians were once hopeful movie stars who never made it, so the next best thing is the political limelight where jealousy and selfish ambition are the ruling traits. What type of government do you think such people would produce? The kind we have, maybe?

Disorder can be seen in everything they say and do. There has never been a government more bloated and complicated than our federal government. It takes months or years to accomplish what should be a common-sense, simple task, (if it is accomplished at all) and with an outrageous price tag.

Her leaders pronounce judgment for a bribe, her priests instruct for a price, and her prophets divine for money. Yet they lean on the Lord saying, "Is not the Lord in our midst? Calamity will not come upon us." (Micah 3:11) *Holding to a form of godliness, although they have denied its power.* (II Timothy 3:5)

The cases of fraud and bribery among elected officials are probably too numerous to be numbered, "yet they lean on the Lord," earnestly stating their case and promoting themselves as righteous God-fearing individuals, begging for a second chance.

Many politicians make sure they are seen walking in and out of church on Sunday morning, carrying their Bible, but it is likely a book they know little about. *"You will know them by their fruits,"* says that book. (Matthew 7:16) Jesus also said, *"wisdom is vindicated by her deeds"* (Matthew 11:19), telling us that the measuring stick of a person's character is his deeds.

They hold to a form of godliness but refuse to honor God by failing to expose the myth of "separation of church and state." The cowardly congressmen duck the issue entirely by passing it off to the Supreme Court, allowing the ungodly members of that body to rule God out of everything. Yet, when a national disaster occurs, those do-nothing legislators are among the first to call for a national day of prayer and can be seen filing in and out of the nearest church, looking so humble.

And they have healed the brokenness of My people superficially, saying, 'peace, peace,' but there is no peace. (Jeremiah 6:14)

Around the middle of the twentieth century liberal government took upon itself the task of creating utopia for its citizens. Severe economic and social problems made the undertaking acceptable to the general public, who have made it a habit of turning to the federal government for every perceived need imaginable.

In the 1930s, the great depression enabled President Roosevelt to make a giant leap forward in establishing the federal government as an all-encompassing soup kitchen -- a liberal dream. FDR's New Deal would make everything right, and he was seen as the savior of our country, but only now are historians acknowledging that it was World War II that saved the economy, not the many alphabet programs of FDR, which actually extended the depression. But the taxes, regulations, and increased power of government remained and continues to grow unchecked to this day.

The social unrest of the fifties and sixties, based on race relations, opened the door for the federal government to launch a multitude of bureaucracies, departments and freedom-sapping laws and regulations. Not satisfied with just helping black Americans with a hand up, the government began seeking ways to help everyone with any problem, eliminating all danger from the lives of Americans, protecting us from ourselves.

Much has been spoken and written by conservatives about the failures of all that help but it hasn't deterred the government from applying it, and now it doesn't even prevent the people from demanding it. All of their solutions to bring peace and tranquility to our lives only creates more pain and suffering. Peace, peace, but there is no peace.

For even your brothers and the household of your father, even they have dealt treacherously with you, even they have cried aloud after you. Do not believe them, although they may say nice things to you. (Jeremiah 12:6)

Our "brothers," the people we vote into office, treat us as children, or, in the least, morons. They think we will believe anything they say and not remember all the promises that never played out. They ascribe no common sense to us nor give us any powers of deduction. All we hear is political speak – the same old worn out clichés that bounce around like a ricocheting bullet when they are asked a difficult question.

The "household of your father" can be likened to the Presidential administration. It is becoming increasingly more difficult to find a candidate of any party who is worthy of being voted into that office. They cry out for our votes, spending hundreds of millions of dollars on campaign messages filled with deceit, assuring us that they have the answers to the problems. But hear God's word – "do not believe them, although they may say nice things to you."

Concerning evil, both hands do it well. The prince asks, also the judge, for a bribe, and a great man speaks the desire of his soul; so they weave it together. (Micah 7:3) It used to be that the conservative Republican party tried to hold onto the values of older times, but nowadays it seems they are more than willing to follow the same path of the liberal Democrats. Godly folks spurned the liberal left and supported the righteous right, but now it is as though we are watching both hands work the deceitful shell game. It doesn't matter under which shell the pea turns up – we're still going to choke on it.

Woe to the rebellious children, declares the Lord, who execute a plan, but not Mine, and make an alliance, but not of My Spirit, in order to add sin to sin; (Isaiah 30:1)

The founders of our country, from George Washington to Ben Franklin, acknowledged a sovereign God and often entreated Him to lead them in the path of righteousness. The plan of the revolution was to make men free and the alliance of the States was to create a country where men could freely worship the God of Heaven, mainly through the Christian religion. The rewriters of history and the authors of the ungodly liberal agenda are the rebellious children who will follow any savior but Jesus.

The prophets prophesy falsely, and the priests rule on their own authority; and My people love it so! But what will you do at the end of it? (Jeremiah 5:31) The prophets and the priests are like the congressmen and the judges. The congressmen tell us how favorable things will be with them in office, and the judges take it upon themselves to pronounce rulings that go against the Constitution and tear down the boundaries of common sense. While a token outrage bounces off each ungodly issue, complacency and apathy rule the day, allowing the deceivers to continue in their ungodliness. But what will we do at the end of it? More importantly, how close are we to the end of it? Judging from the moral condition of our government, we're very close to that time. Might God be weighing us in the balance as He did with His own people, Israel? Might we lose our sovereign country as Old Testament Israel lost theirs? May it be that we are one nation under God.

Taxes

(6) For because of this (subjection) you also pay taxes, for rulers are servants of God, devoting themselves to this very thing. (7) Render to all what is due them: tax to whom tax is due; custom to whom custom; fear to whom fear; honor to whom honor. (Romans 13:6,7)

The Pharisees tried to trap Jesus in the matter of taxes, asking if they should pay Caesar's poll-tax or not, to which He answered, "*render to Caesar the things that are Caesar's, and to God the things that are God's.*" (Mark 12:17)

At another time Peter was asked if his Master paid the two-drachma tax. After a short dissertation on freemen and slaves, Jesus told him to go to the sea and catch a fish. It would have a coin in its mouth that would be sufficient to pay the tax for both Peter and Jesus. (Matthew 17:24-27)

The point of those two instances is that we should meet our secular obligations as well as our godly ones and God will provide for all of our needs if we are trusting in Him.

Any people who are subject to a secular government will have to pay taxes. A Democratic government is not engaged in commercial activity and produces no product, thereby making taxation a necessary source of income. Taxing the citizens is okay with God but how much and for what reason is another matter.

In a perfect world, it is as Romans 13:6 says: "*… rulers are servants of God, devoting themselves to this very thing.*" We have already seen that God allows whomever He pleases to rule a country, and, if they are God-fearing leaders, their chief concern will be to rule according to the principles of God which will benefit the citizens.

Perhaps a moment should be taken to understand just how God benefits His people and gets them what they need. A good explanation can be found in Luke 6:38. *Give, and it will be given to you; good measure, pressed down, shaken together, running over, they will pour into your lap. For by your standard of measure it will be measured to you in return.*

It has always been said that it is better to give than to receive and this verse shows that God's showers of blessings start with our charitable giving. The interesting part of the verse is where it says "they will pour into your lap." Who are "they?" In the King James version the word "men" gives us further explanation. God uses the material wealth of the men of this earth to bless His people and make provision for them.

While all men have free will to do as they please with whatever they have, God can still influence them to do things in a certain way that results in blessings for others. It doesn't matter whether the man is sitting in the oval office, the Senate or House of Representatives, or a State House, there can be divinely influenced decisions made that cause a benefit to shower down upon certain folks at the right time.

This same process works just as well in corporate board rooms, company planning sessions, financial transactions and start-up or shut-down decisions. The irony of it is that God can use the same action to benefit one while bringing chastisement upon another. At any rate, we can see that God uses men for His purpose.

Going back to Romans 13:7, and remembering that God gives us whatever kind of government we deserve, we receive instruction to pay any tax levied upon us. We are to pay "tax to whom tax is due," but the government would do well to remember that in the early days of our country, taxes were to be collected mainly through tariffs; that is, on goods imported from other countries.

For our first hundred years we were spared the burdensome task of paying a tax on everything under the sun, but in 1913 the income tax went into effect for all time. It started as do all government programs – a little at a time. Just 1%. That wouldn't really hurt anyone. And to make it really easy for us, they would just go ahead and deduct that amount from our paychecks.

The main reason for the payroll deduction was so that we wouldn't have to write out a check to pay that tax on a regular basis, getting angrier every time we looked at that amount. If the government takes it before we even cash our paycheck, we never have it in the first place. Also, the payroll deduction makes it easier to raise the tax rate from time to time without anyone noticing. It may be called a deduction or a contribution, but it is still confiscation.

You shall not charge interest to your countrymen: interest on money, food, or anything that may be loaned at interest. (20) You may charge interest to a foreigner, but to your countryman you shall not charge interest ... (Deuteronomy 23:19, 20)

If it was wrong for the people engaged in commerce and finance to charge interest to their countrymen, how can it be right for a government to lay excessive taxes upon its people? Just as interest was to be charged to the foreigner, that's where the bulk of taxes should be levied. Does God not notice when governments lay heavy taxation burdens upon its people? *Thus says the Lord God, "Enough, you princes of Israel; put away violence and destruction, and practice justice and righteousness. Stop your expropriations from My people," declares the Lord God.* (Ezekiel 45:9)

The NASB uses "expropriations" while the KJV uses "exactings" to describe the wickedness. To expropriate is to take land from its owner for public use. Exacting is making severe demands. Both translations are good words to describe our government's actions toward us, especially in the area of taxation and God's response to it.

Tell the sons of Israel to raise a contribution for Me; from every man whose heart moves him you shall raise My contribution. Exodus (25:2) That is the spirit in which men should give to anyone for anything. It should be a "contribution" from the heart. A recent President liked to call taxes "contributions," but a heavy-handed IRS cared not whether it came from the heart or was forcibly taken from the paycheck.

Well, how much should we pay? And who should pay? God says everyone should pay and it should be the same amount. In Exodus 30:11-16, God told Moses that the atonement money (a half shekel) would be paid by anyone 20 years old or older, and they all would pay the same amount. *The rich shall not pay more, and the poor shall not pay less than the half shekel, when you give the contribution to the Lord to make atonement for yourselves.* (verse 15)

Someone may say that this passage is about atonement for sin and has nothing to do with paying government taxes, but our federal government treats us as sinners, and the only way we can escape punishment is to make atonement by payment of our income taxes.

We are taxed in percentages of our income, not a certain amount of dollars, and that is the fairest way to do it. If everyone had to pay an income tax of say, $1,000 a year, that wouldn't be fair because a thousand dollars to a man making ten thousand a year is a greater burden than for a man making a million dollars a year. It would be no burden at all on the million dollar earner.

The percentage method raises a substantial amount of revenue without burdening anyone as long as it is a manageable percentage and it is the same percentage for everyone. One of the great deceptions of our time is the rich supposedly not paying their fair share. If the percentage was the same for everyone, the rich would still be paying more than the middle class or those below the poverty line, because they would be paying a percentage of a much larger amount.

God says the rich shall not pay more and the poor shall not pay less for atonement; why should it be any different for government revenue? And what should the percentage be? Abraham paid a tenth to Melchizadek, the priest, (Genesis 14:20) and Jacob vowed to God that he would give back a tenth of all he received. (Genesis 28:22) The Levites had the *... commandment in the Law to collect a tenth from the people, that is, from their brethren ...* (Hebrews 7:5) If ten percent is good enough for God, why isn't it good enough for the government?

Men prepare a meal for enjoyment, and wine makes life merry, and money is the answer to everything. (Ecclesiastes 10:19) That verse describes our times as much as any other verse in the Bible. Our freedom has produced an abundance that is unequaled anywhere in the world or at any time in history. Our desire of entitlement has us focusing on material goods and pleasures and falsely believing the federal government has the capacity and the money to provide it all.

That way of thinking is responsible for our current high tax rates and the counsel of politicians in the liberal Democratic party who tell us that it is necessary to raise taxes even more. They present themselves as the ones who can bless us in the place of God. They help us by redistributing wealth through taxation but ignore a basic fact.

That is, when taxes are raised, the economy suffers, and that is because when people are taxed excessively they will tend to hold onto the money that is left. The lower income people will spend less and the upper income folks will stop investing and expanding their businesses. If someone is going to be penalized more for working harder and taking greater business risks, they usually back away from such activity. And if folks have less in the paycheck, they will have less to spend.

It's a snowball effect that has been well documented by economists. When taxes are raised, the economy suffers and actually less revenue is collected. When taxes are lowered, there is an economic boom with much higher revenue flowing into the treasury. But it is not what the liberal politicians, mainly in the Democratic party, want you to understand. They want you to believe that they need the higher tax rates to meet your needs, but they need those rates to maintain their control over your life.

John 12:6 gives us an understanding of Judas Iscariot's motives when he complained to Jesus about a woman wasting expensive perfume, which could have been sold and the money used to help the poor, or so he said. *Now he said this, not because he was concerned about the poor, but because he was a thief, and as he had the money box, he used to pilfer what was put into it.*

A good description of our state and federal politicians who care nothing for those in need; they only care for our money and their careers.

Suppression

When the righteous increase, the people rejoice, but when a wicked man rules, people groan. (Proverbs 29:2) Sometimes, when I read a verse such as this one, I wonder why it is included in a book of wisdom. It's such a common sense, simple statement, it should be something that everybody knows. Why do we have to be told? The answer lies within human nature. Righteous people tend to get complacent when things go well, and wicked men are always looking to gain a hand up on the masses.

But what is righteousness? Who is a righteous person? Psalm 24:3-5 answers those questions very well. (3) *Who may ascend into the hill of the Lord? And who may stand in His holy place?* (4) *He who has clean hands and a pure heart, who has not lifted up his soul to falsehood, and has not sworn deceitfully.* (5) *He shall receive a blessing from the Lord and righteousness from the God of his salvation.*

It's a two for two trade-off. Clean hands and a pure heart is in – falsehood and deceit is out. Those four things are the basis of righteousness. Get two – get rid of two.

God imputes righteousness to:

1. a person with clean hands; that is, one who is honest in all his doings.

2. one who has a pure heart; whose thoughts are only of godliness.

3. one who does not deal with other men, or God, on a basis of falsehood.

4. one who does not deceive other men for personal gain.

Such a man will receive righteousness from God.

Now, wouldn't you think that righteousness would be the first qualification listed in the requirements for serving in a position of government? Especially the office of President? Who wouldn't want an honest, upright man to serve as the leader of our country? Well, a lot of folks don't. At least, that's how they vote after they are told by the liberal media of the dangers of electing some religious radical to the presidency who will force everyone to carry their Bible to church every Sunday morning. They warn the voters of the dangers of electing such a man, with slanted remarks directed at his beliefs, implying that he will impose all kinds of religious restrictions upon the people, breaking down the barrier that separates church from state and who knows what all.

In a democracy, righteous people will always flourish, making the country better off as a whole. But with Satan blinding the minds of so many people, the righteous are seen as a threat. It is very difficult for a truly righteous person to get elected to any high office. Perhaps that is why the people end up groaning more than rejoicing.

And they tie up heavy loads, and lay them on men's shoulders; but they themselves are unwilling to move them with so much as a finger. (Matthew 23:4)

The scope of our federal government is astounding. There are more laws than any one person can know about. There are more Departments than necessary. There are more Bureaucracies than needed. One good example of the complicated confusion is the IRS tax code which prevents most people from being able to fill out an income tax form.

We have been tied up with such a heavy load that we may never be able to get out from under it. As average citizens, there is no way we can. Only righteous people serving in Congress have the wherewithal to relieve the burden. The ones who are there now care nothing about these problems. It actually is a positive for them, in that it makes it harder for us to figure out what they are doing. The populace can speak forever on the problems of our country and what should be done about it; the candidates can make a promise to cover every issue, but the incumbent rules and does not lift a finger to help.

In the book of Nehemiah, the Israelites, following their return from exile to Jerusalem, are lamenting their condition. On a certain day, dressed in sackcloth and ashes, they separated themselves from all foreigners and stood and confessed their sins to God and read from the book of the Law, and said:

Behold, we are slaves today, and as to the land which Thou didst give to our fathers to eat of its fruit and its bounty, behold, we are slaves on it. And its abundant produce is for the kings whom Thou hast set over us because of our sins; they also rule over our bodies and over our cattle as they please, so we are in great distress. (Nehemiah 9:36-37)

America, the land of the free. If you compare the heavy-handed rule and regulation of today with that as it was at the beginning of our nation, you may come to believe we are in the same boat as those old Israelites. What with property taxes and the law of eminent domain, our property is not really ours, and can be taken from us for public use any time the government chooses.

Our abundant produce is gobbled up in taxes to feed the bloated government departments and bureaucracies and the pork barrel projects of the legislators. They rule over us as they please, passing whatever law gets them good notice in the liberal press and votes on the next election day.

Notice also how they rule over our bodies in deciding what we can eat or drink and do or not do. This is all done in the name of protectionism and consumer safety in their quest to rule our lives from cradle to grave.

How did we get to this point? Well, it didn't happen in the last few years. It started back in the 1930s during the great depression and the administration of Franklin Delano Roosevelt. 1936 marked the end of FDR's first term and in June the Republicans gathered in Cleveland for their national convention, determined to make it his last term. On Friday, June 12, the GOP platform appeared on the front page of the New York Times and read as follows:

(Quote) America is in peril. The welfare of American men and women and the future of our youth are at stake. We dedicate ourselves to the preservation of their political liberty, their individual opportunity and their character as free citizens, which today for the first time are threatened by government itself.

For three long years the New Deal administration has dishonored American traditions and flagrantly betrayed the pledges upon which the Democratic party sought and received public support.

The powers of Congress have been usurped by the President.

The integrity and authority of the Supreme Court have been flaunted.

The rights and liberties of American citizens have been violated.

Regulated monopoly has displaced free enterprise.

The New Deal administration constantly seeks to usurp the rights reserved to the State and to the people.

It has insisted on passage of laws contrary to the Constitution.

It has intimidated witnesses and interfered with the right of petition.

It has dishonored our country by repudiating its most sacred obligations.

It has been guilty of frightful waste and extravagance, using public funds for partisan political purposes.

It has promoted investigations to harass and intimidate American citizens, at the same time denying investigations into its own improper expenditures.

It has created a vast multitude of new offices, filled them with its favorites, set up a centralized bureaucracy and sent out swarms of inspectors to harass our people.

It has bred fear and hesitation in commerce and industry, thus discouraging new enterprises, preventing employment and prolonging the depression.

It secretly has made tariff agreements with our foreign competitors, flooding our markets with foreign commodities.

It has coerced and intimidated voters by withholding relief to those opposing its tyrannical policies.

It has destroyed the morale of many of our people and made them dependent upon government.

Appeals to passion and class prejudice have replaced reason and tolerance.

To a free people, these actions are insufferable. This campaign cannot be waged on the traditional differences between the Republican and Democratic parties.

The responsibility of this election transcends all previous political divisions. We invite all Americans, irrespective of party, to join us in defense of American institutions.
(End of quote)

So, there it is. What we are experiencing today with our government has been going on for over 70 years. The problems are deep rooted and won't likely be changed in a few years. Almost all of the statements from that party platform could be used to describe our condition today. We are a people in the greatest free nation on earth, and yet, we are in a state of suppression under the largest government on earth.

It has been said that God gives people the kind of government they deserve, and maybe we deserve the corrupt government we have today, but even though God will allow a somewhat nasty government to be in power for the chastisement of the people, He will not approve of its methods and not allow it to go unpunished for its many injustices.

The Lord enters into judgment with the elders and princes of His people, "It is you who have devoured the vineyard; the plunder of the poor is in your houses. "What do you mean by crushing My people, and grinding the face of the poor?" declares the Lord God of hosts. (Isaiah 3:14-15)

Remedy

And what are we to do about all of this? God gives instruction, but it takes courage to act righteously.

For there are many rebellious men, empty talkers and deceivers, especially those of the circumcision, (11) who must be silenced because they are upsetting whole families, teaching things they should not teach, for the sake of sordid gain. (Titus 1:10-11)

In his letter to Titus, the apostle Paul instructs him on how to handle offenders in the church. It has been said, though not Biblical, that God helps those who help themselves. If we are not willing to speak out against immorality, injustice, and general ungodliness, can we really expect God to do anything on our behalf?

Paul describes the offenders in verse 10 and pays special attention to "those of the circumcision." They were the Jews who professed to know God but brushed aside the total work of Christ on the cross, teaching that circumcision was still a necessary step in salvation. Paul would have none of that. They were wrong and should be silenced because of the trouble and confusion they were causing. There was no consideration of free speech.

Today, in our weakness and in our attempt to show Christian love, we have allowed great intrusions in our faith. We excuse our failure to respond by insisting we are merely complying with the rights of individuals as guaranteed in the Constitution, not wanting to be labeled as religious fanatics or right-wing extremists.

But truth is truth, and if we believe our religion of Christianity is the only path to salvation and eternal life, there should be no tolerance or compromise for any other teaching. No one will draw a line for fear of being accused of intolerance, bigotry, and a lack of sensitivity. But God draws lines. He drew a line for Adam and Eve, He drew lines for the Israelites and the heathen countries, He has drawn a line with Jesus Christ and He will draw a very straight line at the end of the age. If you are a born-again believer, you already saw the line He drew for you, and you stepped onto the right side of that line.

Free speech is a cherished right but no one has the right to speak that which is harmful to others in the matter of morality and eternal life. Why does the surgeon and his assistants wear masks in the operating room? Don't they have the right to breathe freely? Yes, but it would not be wise to allow their germs to float around and enter the body of the patient, causing an infection that could prove fatal. Shouldn't we take the same precautions against immorality and false religious teaching? Shouldn't we keep advising certain people to "shut up" in spite of whatever names we are called?

If anyone comes to you and does not bring this teaching, do not receive him into your house, and do not give him a greeting; (11) for the one who gives him a greeting participates in his evil deeds. (2 John 10, 11)

The apostle John wrote this short letter to a fellow Christian with some cautions concerning false teachers. John flatly states in verse nine that the only true teaching involves the work of Christ and he warns the believer in the following verses that if anyone comes around with a different teaching, he should not be allowed into the house, or even met with a greeting. To not even give a greeting indicates the seriousness of the issue and the dangers of fraternizing with such persons.

What about the ungodly politicians who greet us and tell us nice things, but shy away from acknowledging God as sovereign and Christ as the Savior of the world? If we're not supposed to allow them in our house, or even give them a greeting, should we give them our vote? Many otherwise good Christians are fooled into doing just that by the sweet promise of entitlements. Political corruption will never end as long as Christians keep voting for ungodly liberals because of what the Democratic party meant to them fifty years ago. The liberal Democrats keep making promises on situations that no longer exist, and too many people haven't taken the time to figure it out. The scariest part of it is some supposedly conservative Republicans are beginning to follow the liberal ways. God help us.

You shall not follow a multitude in doing evil, nor shall you testify in a dispute so as to turn aside after a multitude in order to pervert justice; (Exodus 23:2)

This was the instruction God gave to Moses for the people of Israel. They were not to get caught up in the frenzy of a crowd and follow a way that was not God's way. They were to be a discerning people who would measure the issues of the day with God's word. Christians should not be deceived by the pronouncements of the liberal media and the smooth words of ungodly politicians.

The primary elections in the early part of a presidential election year are an example of how the candidates try to stampede the voters toward their camp by winning a few contests in small, mostly irrelevant states.

And do not participate in the unfruitful deeds of darkness, but instead even expose them; (Ephesians 5:11)

After warning the people against immorality, impurity, and covetousness, Paul sums up with that statement. It doesn't matter how popular some things are; it doesn't matter that conventional wisdom says follow the crowd. Jesus never gave the Pharisees an inch. He never bent in the slightest toward their position. They were wrong and He was right. Why would He compromise God's word to satisfy their lust for power and the pursuit of evil? Why do we?

For the Lord has rejected those in whom you trust, and you shall not prosper with them. (Jeremiah 2:37)

Chapter Eight

ABORTION

Deceives Mankind into Self-annihilation

To this point we have seen how Satan has been influencing the minds of people to turn away from God in descending fashion. At the top of the ladder is a simple suggestion that there is no God. Then, in a perversion of our sexuality, the devil has misrepresented the masculine authority of God and our race, and twisted the man-woman sexual relationship into one of same sex.

For those who failed to be taken in by such wickedness, Satan offered the option of animal and earth worship, dropping down a few more rungs on the morality ladder from human compromises to glorifying the creature and inanimate objects.

His most damaging efforts have been in our education system where our young people are being indoctrinated with teaching on atheism, feminism, homosexuality, animal rights, and the environment. If Satan can captivate a young person with ungodly teaching, it will be much easier to influence that person as an adult.

Another major victory has been in promoting government as the answer to all problems and as the provider for all needs. But with abortion, we have reached the bottom of that ladder by believing Satan's lie that life in the womb is not sacred and can be legally extinguished with the flimsiest of excuses. If he can't destroy us within his limitations, he can influence us to destroy ourselves.

Stalin killed over twenty million in Russia. Hitler killed six million through severe persecution of the Jewish people. The abortion clinics in America have killed fifty million. Such outrages can be understood in the light of the Communist revolution and the Nazi purge, but in peaceful America? If God condemned different nations in Old Testament times for slaughtering the innocent, what must He be thinking of us?

There is not a nation in history that has continued long after committing genocide. Germany, after its persecution of the Jews and responsibility for millions of other World War II deaths, went down in flames with all of the perpetrators meeting justice. The powerful Soviet Union that brought death and suffering to so many, crumbled into a singular, second-rate power, whose final judgment is yet to come. How can America escape such an end by its ruling of death for the infant in the womb?

The liberal argument on abortion is the same as the other ungodly issues of their agenda. They create new words for old procedures and give new meaning to old words, but the procedures are what they are and the words mean what they always meant. It is abortion, not pro-choice. Aborting the pregnancy is killing the child in the womb. Women's rights do not include the right to choose death for an innocent child. A woman has the right to decide the course for her own body, but the body in her womb is not her body.

Concerning a baby, a woman has a definite choice on two occasions. The first is when she chooses to have or not have sex. The second is after the baby leaves her womb, when she can choose to keep it as her own or allow it to be adopted by loving parents who would nurture the child as God intended. It's her choice, and no one can take it away from her. If she chooses not to have sex that may result in pregnancy, there is no problem for anyone. If she chooses to engage in sexual activity that brings pregnancy, she has the remaining choice of adoption after delivery, which is a benefit to her, the baby, and the adopting parents. Nobody gets hurt.

Don't you think it odd that laws prevent us from killing certain creatures of the wild, even though doing so is for beneficial reasons, yet the law protects the woman who wants to kill the tiny human in her womb? If a woman can kill the creature within her body for her own benefit, why can't the landowner kill the creature for the beneficial use of his own land? It's a classic example of liberal hypocrisy and further demonstration of Satan's power of deception.

Life

For the life of the flesh is in the blood, and I have given it to you on the altar to make atonement for your souls; for it is the blood by reason of the life that makes atonement. (Leviticus 17:11)

Yes, this statement was made 3500 years ago to a people engaged in a religion of animal sacrifice, but the distance of time and the method of worship does nothing to lessen the truth of the statement. God is a God who changes not, and His word is not annulled by one who chooses not to believe.

God was explaining to the Israelites that the life of the flesh is in the blood and there is no remission of sins without the shedding of blood. God could have created our bodies in any form imaginable with any type of makeup involving matter and organs. In order to emphasize the importance of life and the sustaining element thereof, He created the circulatory system which carries our blood throughout our bodies bringing life to every cell. Without the blood, a cell will die. Without the blood, a body will die.

God accepted the shedding of human blood in only two instances – one in general, and the other, special. The general instance is in the carrying out of the death penalty for blasphemy against God and wickedness against a fellow human being. The special instance was in the shedding of Christ's blood for the atonement of sin. There was no other acceptance for the shedding of blood.

Well, what does this have to do with abortion? The point is, every infant in the womb is sustained by human blood from the time of conception; first by the mother's blood and shortly thereafter by its own circulatory system as development progresses. The infant is not a mere fetus or tissue mass; it is a human being created in a wondrous fashion ordained by God, its life sustained by the blood of life flowing through its veins. *For as for the life of all flesh, its blood is identified with its life.* (Lev. 17:14)

In the book of James there's a passage explaining the relationship of faith and works. He concludes by saying, *For just as the body without the spirit is dead, so also faith without works is dead.* (2:26)

James uses the illustration of body and spirit for faith and works, and he wouldn't use as an illustration something that wasn't true or had no meaning. The body without the spirit is dead; that's a fact, just as the body without the blood is dead. Every human body has a natural sustainer (blood) and a supernatural sustainer (spirit). The presence of man's spirit is the overriding proof of human life.

In John, 3:13, Jesus said, "*and no one has ascended into heaven, but He who descended from heaven, even the Son of Man.*"

That statement would indicate that no one on earth has ever been in heaven except Jesus. His reasoning isn't just that no man has gone into heaven, but that no man knows anything about heaven because no one has ever been there. In the preceding verse Jesus said that man could not understand anything He spoke about heaven because there was a lack of familiarity on man's part.

But is Jesus talking about the physical human body being in heaven previously? No, because His physical human body was not in heaven. He was in heaven as a spirit, and He is saying no one on earth was ever in heaven in spirit form. Man is given a spirit that contains his consciousness; his awareness. It is the spirit that energizes the body, particularly the mind.

Just as electricity flowing through a wire produces a surrounding magnetic field, the presence of the spirit creates the aura of life in our bodies. The spirit is in the body at the moment of conception, else there would be no life. As long as the spirit is within man, the man lives. When the spirit departs, the body dies, just as the magnetic field collapses when the current ceases to flow in the wire. Jesus' body died when He gave up the spirit on the cross of Calvary.

Consider this possibility for the beginning of a person's spirit. Our spirit could come into existence the same way as our physical body. There is the life of the mother in the egg and the life of the father in the sperm cell. If our spirit is what gives life to the physical body, wouldn't the spirits of the parents be combined in the first cell of the infant, enabling that fertilized egg to be alive?

A human being is not created from nothing. Before the egg and sperm unite, they are alive in their host bodies. Actually, there is no special moment of physical creation when a baby is formed – "formed" being the key word. God uses that word when He speaks of our beginning in Isaiah 44:24a, *Thus says the Lord, your Redeemer, and the one who formed you from the womb ...*

The material God uses to form each body is already there, just as the material for Eve was in Adam's rib. And just as there is no combustion without oxygen, the egg does nothing until the sperm cell shows up and adds its DNA to the scene, sparking the growth. Then, with the pattern originally formed in Adam, the wisdom of God in the double-helix of DNA begins to weave a new human being. This has been happening for 6,000 years without man even knowing there was such a thing as DNA.

Since each physical body is merely the continuation of the physical life of the parents, wouldn't it seem logical that the spirits of those parents combine with the joining of the sperm and egg and begin a new spirit in the same way those two physical cells begin a new physical body? That would better explain how the original sin of Adam has been passed on through the entire human race. His carnal spirit has been passed on, the same as his body. It would also explain why most children have the same mannerisms as their parents.

So how was Jesus born without sin? *" ... The Holy Spirit will come upon you, and the power of the Most High will overshadow you; and for that reason the holy offspring shall be called the Son of God."* (Luke 1:35)

Those were the words of the angel Gabriel as he announced to the virgin Mary that a child would be conceived in her womb. However, it would be the total work of the Holy Spirit. There would be no contribution of an egg from Mary or a sperm from Joseph. And that is why Jesus was born without sin.

There was no human sperm cell or egg that carried the spirit of an earthly father or mother into Mary's womb. In the only act of creation that was ever performed in any womb, a male sperm and a female egg, with appropriate DNA was created to begin a new human body. The spirit of the second person of the Holy Trinity was inserted into that tiny, two-celled human being to become the only child of God.

And it came about that when Elizabeth heard Mary's greeting, the baby leaped in her womb; and Elizabeth was filled with the Holy Spirit. (Luke 1:41) After the Virgin Mary became pregnant she visited her relative, Elizabeth, who was already pregnant with the infant John, who would become the famous "Baptist," the forerunner of Christ.

When Mary entered the house, the baby in Elizabeth's womb leaped for joy at the sound of Mary's voice. The spirit of John was reveling, knowing that the spirit of Christ was in the same room. The point is, God did not influence Luke to say that the "fetus" moved, or the "viable tissue mass" experienced a convulsion. The *baby* leaped in her womb.

A second point is that a not-yet-human fetus, or a tissue mass, is not capable of responding to an idea instigated by a spoken word. The pro-death group apparently does not believe the pre-born infant has a spirit because none of them have dealt with the question of what happens to the aborted baby's spirit. Admitting to a pre-born spirit would place them in an extremely unpopular position and one that is indefensible. That is why they don't want to admit that it is a living human being, and also why they don't even want to mention the word death in the procedure or the debate.

How was the "spirit-less tissue mass" in Elizabeth's womb able to recognize a voice and comprehend the meaning? John the Baptist and Jesus Christ began life on earth as two-cell human beings. The awareness of those pre-born infants proves that life in the womb is greater and more real than any life produced by mere evolution.

Think about it. While the evolutionists say that it took millions of years for the cells of living creatures to evolve into the mammals of today, the abortionists are saying it only takes seconds for the subject to evolve from a tissue mass to a verifiable living human being. How else do you explain partial birth abortion?

The healthy baby's body, except for the head, can be outside the body of the mother when the abortionist kills the child. It would only take another second for the head to clear the birth canal, bringing entire separation. So, we are asked to believe that the tissue mass suddenly becomes a human being with rights in just one second. Can any doctor or scientist tell us what happened in that tiny body in that one second that brought about such a change in status? You see, from the abortion standpoint, the question of life and when it begins doesn't matter; it about position — whether it is inside or out of the mother's body.

The fact that so many intelligent people can be so blinded to the truth and so wrong, is evidence of the supernatural influence of Satan. If plain old common sense prevailed, without even bringing morality into it, the abortion issue would never have gotten off the ground. Oh, for the days of common sense and when we believed such statements as Psalm 127:3 which said, *"Behold, children are a gift of the Lord; the fruit of the womb is a reward."*

The abortionists are throwing the gift of the Lord back in His face.

Foreknowledge

For Thou didst form my inward parts; Thou didst weave me in my mother's womb. I will give thanks to Thee, for I am fearfully and wonderfully made; wonderful are Thy works, and my soul knows it very well. My frame was not hidden from Thee, when I was made in secret, and skillfully wrought in the depths of the earth. Thine eyes have seen my unformed substance; and in Thy book they were all written, the days that were ordained for me, when as yet there was not one of them. (Psalm 139:13-16)

This passage confirms the omniscience of God. He knows everything about us. He even knew us before we existed in earthly form. He knows what our beginning was and what our end shall be. *"Before I formed you in the womb I knew you, ... "* (Jeremiah 1:5)

The prophet Isaiah was also made aware of God's foreknowledge of each of us. *"Thus says the Lord who made you and formed you from the womb, ... "* (44:2)

The scriptures are not silent on the abortion debate. For any who choose to believe, God gives the instruction and leaves no doubt as to when life begins and how sacred it is. Not only does God know of us before our earthly existence, He has plans for each of us as noted by Paul, Isaiah, and Jeremiah.

But when He who had set me apart, even from my mother's womb, and called me through His grace, was pleased (Galatians 1:15)

Listen to me, O islands, and pay attention, you peoples from afar. The Lord called Me from the womb; from the body of My mother He named Me. (Isaiah 49:1)

And now says the Lord, who formed Me from the womb to be His Servant ... (Isaiah 49:5) (a reference to Christ)

... and before you were born I consecrated you; ... (Jeremiah 1:5)

In God's intentions for good He gives each of us a purpose. If we are obedient to God and live according to His commandments, those good intentions will be realized. But if we thwart those intentions, as in abortion, we are missing out on great blessings and will earn at least, severe chastisement from God, if not full wrath.

It is often said that among the millions killed by abortion, there may be many who would have been a blessing to our country in the way of new inventions, cures for diseases, and countless methods of humanitarian assistance. We often pray that God would send us good leaders, but did we kill them while they were still in the womb?

Selection

And he said, "When you are helping the Hebrew women to give birth and see them upon the birthstool, if it is a son, then you shall put him to death; but if it is a daughter, then she shall live." (Exodus 1:16)

This was Pharaoh's command to the midwives when assisting in an Israelite birth.

The time of Joseph was past and the Egyptians no longer looked favorably upon the Israelites, enslaving them in response to their fears of this growing people in their land. The idea was to treat them badly, forcing them to serve as slave labor in making national improvements, also expecting it to exact a great toll on the Israelites' health and well-being, causing death and a gradual decrease in their population. That has always been the final solution for any unwanted people in history and it goes on today.

A daughter born to an Israelite was acceptable as she would grow up to be a good servant, not posing any threat. But Pharaoh made a pre-emptive strike concerning the boys. If they weren't alive, they could not be a threat of any kind. However, after the midwives refused to carry out Pharaoh's evil instructions he ordered the parents to throw every son born into the Nile River.

Such extreme measures of birth control are in the world today. China has severely limited the family size in order to control their huge population, forcing abortion on most women. But isn't it odd that here brought about such a change in status? You see, from the abortionists' standpoint, the question of life and when it begins doesn't matter; it is all about position – whether it is inside or out of the mother's body.

The fact that so many intelligent people can be so blinded to the truth and so wrong, is evidence of the supernatural influence of Satan. If plain old common sense prevailed, without even bringing morality into it, the abortion issue would never have gotten off the ground. Oh, for the days of common sense and when we believed such statements as Psalm 127:3 which said, *"Behold, children are a gift of the Lord; the fruit of the womb is a reward."*

The abortionists are throwing the gift of the Lord back in His face.

Foreknowledge

For Thou didst form my inward parts; Thou didst weave me in my mother's womb. I will give thanks to Thee, for I am fearfully and wonderfully made; wonderful are Thy works, and my soul knows it very well. My frame was not hidden from Thee, when I was made in secret, and skillfully wrought in the depths of the earth. Thine eyes have seen my unformed substance; and in Thy book they were all written, the days that were ordained for me, when as yet there was not one of them. (Psalm 139:13-16)

This passage confirms the omniscience of God. He knows everything about us. He even knew us before we existed in earthly form. He knows what our beginning was and what our end shall be. *"Before I formed you in the womb I knew you, ... "* (Jeremiah 1:5)

The prophet Isaiah was also made aware of God's foreknowledge of each of us. *"Thus says the Lord who made you and formed you from the womb, ... "* (44:2)

The scriptures are not silent on the abortion debate. For any who choose to believe, God gives the instruction and leaves no doubt as to when life begins and how sacred it is. Not only does God know of us before our earthly existence, He has plans for each of us as noted by Paul, Isaiah, and Jeremiah.

But when He who had set me apart, even from my mother's womb, and called me through His grace, was pleased (Galatians 1:15)

Listen to me, O islands, and pay attention, you peoples from afar. The Lord called Me from the womb; from the body of My mother He named Me. (Isaiah 49:1) in America, where there is no problem of a too-large population, over one million abortions take place every year.

Another interesting note is the immigration issue where it is said that the illegal immigrants are necessary to perform certain jobs. The liberals claim that the illegals are merely performing jobs that Americans won't do, but unemployment in early 2008 was at an all-time low, so if some Americans had to start doing those undesirable jobs, who would have filled the positions already occupied by those legal Americans? Abortion has given us an employment problem to which the liberals and conservatives won't admit. Fifty million people could have been added to the population since 1973 were it not for legalized abortion. I'm sure that twelve million (the estimated number of illegal aliens) of those aborted would have been added to the work force.

Abortion is selection in determining who shall live and who shall die. Many different excuses are made for aborting the baby. The mother is an unwed teenager or a career woman. The parents are not yet ready to start raising a family, or, they already have the maximum number of children desired. Or, the most ungodly excuse of claiming to save the child from an unhappy childhood in a poverty-stricken family or community. Talk about playing God and passing judgment!

All life belongs to God and it is to Him alone to decide who lives and who dies and when that happens. The liberals often tell us Christians to not be judgmental but then they go over the top in deciding what kind of future lies in wait for the unborn. There have been many great people who were born into poverty, but overcame through hard work and faith in the grace of God.

If a certain child in the womb is likely to be born into poverty, and we are doing a great humanitarian service by prohibiting that birth, why isn't that tactic applied around the world in the poverty-stricken third-world countries? Why aren't all babies aborted for a few years to relieve the starvation conditions? Why aren't some of the population "aborted" to relieve the problem? Why aren't children with no hope, living in the ghettoes of America "aborted?"

A child is a child on the day before it is born, and a child is a child on the day after it is born. The abortionists don't give public explanations or demonstrations of exactly what takes place in their clinics because of the gruesomeness of the procedure and the media are certainly not going to go looking for it. We can hardly bear to see a man executed under the death penalty; how could we watch a baby being chopped to pieces or having its brains sucked out?

Selection is selfish. It goes against all that God's Word says about how we should treat one another. Jesus gave many lessons on loving one's neighbor. What would He think about killing a child in the womb for personal benefit? The liberal abortionists need to be told that Jesus was against such practices and all judgment has been given to Him. The dealers in death won't have to answer to me or you, but they will answer to Jesus at the final judgment.

For those who think the Bible says nothing on this issue, read Ezekiel 16:4-6 for a look at how God views the birth of an unwanted child.

"As for your birth, on the day you were born your navel cord was not cut, nor were you washed with water for cleansing; you were not rubbed with salt or even wrapped in cloths. No eye looked with pity on you to do any of these things for you, to have compassion on you. Rather you were thrown out into the open field, for you were abhorred on the day you were born. When I passed by you and saw you squirming in your blood, I said to you while you were in your blood, "Live!" I said to you while you were in your blood, "Live!'

This passage speaks of national Israel as an unwanted child, thrown out to die, but rescued by the Lord. If God uses this picture of a shameful birth as an illustration, then it must declare His feelings toward the outrage of abortion. He speaks of pity and compassion on the child squirming in its blood. What must be His position toward those at work in the abortion clinics?

In Deuteronomy 30:19 God sets a life and death choice before the Israelites. *"I call heaven and earth to witness against you today, that I have set before you life and death, the blessing and the curse. So choose life in order that you may live, you and your descendants."*

Nowhere in the scriptures does God allow a loophole for the woman's right to choose an abortion. In selecting when a child will or will not be born, or whether that child will be male or female, or whether that child will be born with a prenatal disease or not, a woman is choosing death for another human being. No getting around it.

Because you have said, "We have made a covenant with death, and with Sheol we have made a pact. The overwhelming scourge will not reach us when it passes by, for we have made falsehood our refuge and we have concealed ourselves with deception." (Isaiah 28:15)

This was God's word to the people of Samaria for making a pact with Assyria rather than trusting in Him. The woman's right to choose, as upheld by the Supreme Court was nothing more than a covenant with death, based on falsehood and deception.

Satan convinced the woman in the garden that she had the right to knowledge that God was trying to withhold, and Satan has convinced the woman of today that she has the right of "choice" for a body that is not hers. The women's lib movement has made a pact with Satan.

Sacrifice

To some, the words of the Bible, especially those of the Old Testament, are nothing more than an account of what happened to some people in ancient times, and quite possibly not even true. They would see no connection between Old Testament Israel and America of today. However, it would be wise to consider that God brought the nation of Israel into existence as a people known by His name; a people special above all other nations in the world.

The most important point is that if He brought judgment and severe chastisement on the people whom He loved, for doing the same kind of things we do in America, wouldn't it follow that the same judgment and chastisement will fall on us as well? We would be extremely naïve to think otherwise.

Okay, so what did Israel do that we are doing that's on the list of God's no-no's? Just what we've been talking about in this chapter -- killing our innocent children.

"Moreover, you took your sons and daughters whom you had borne to Me, and you sacrificed them to idols to be devoured. Were your harlotries so small a matter? You slaughtered My children, and offered them up to idols by causing them to pass through the fire." (Ezekiel 16:20-21)

This is what happens when people turn away from God and begin worshipping false gods and idols. A false god may be a superstition, and an idol may be a manmade graven image, but such things can also be a system or a fleshly desire. The idols of today are selfish desires granted and encouraged by an ungodly system.

Therefore consider the members of your earthly body as dead to immorality, impurity, passion, evil desire, and greed, which amounts to idolatry. (Colossians 3:5)

More than fifty million babies have been offered up to the idols of career, feminism, freedom in pleasure, and the desire of costly material goods. Among all of God's commandments and statutes, not one can be found where He commanded us to sacrifice our children to a false god. It never entered into His mind to put such a requirement upon us.

We have committed adultery with our idol of "freedom of choice," leaving blood on our hands in that we have legalized the abortion of a pregnancy, killing the child in the womb. The Lord says He hates that and commands us to not behave in such a way, confirming that attitude in different times to different people.

And they have built the high places of Topheth, which is in the valley of the son of Hinnom, to burn their sons and their daughters in the fire, which I did not command, and it did not come into My mind. (Jeremiah 7:31)

For they have committed adultery, and blood is on their hands. Thus they have committed adultery with their idols and even caused their sons, whom they bore to Me, to pass through the fire to them as food. (Ezekiel 23:37)

You shall not behave thus toward the Lord your God, for every abominable act which the Lord hates they have done for their gods; for they even burn their sons and daughters in the fire to their gods. (Deuteronomy 12:31)

Penalties

(2) You shall also say to the sons of Israel, 'Any man from the sons of Israel or from the aliens sojourning in Israel, who gives any of his offspring to Molech, shall surely be put to death; the people of the land shall stone him with stones. (3) 'I will also set My face against that man and will cut him off from among his people, because he has given some of his offspring to Molech, so as to defile My sanctuary and to profane My holy name. (4) 'If the people of the land, however, should ever disregard that man when he gives any of his offspring to Molech, so as not to put him to death, (5) then I Myself will set My face against that man and against his family; and I will cut off from among their people both him and all those who play the harlot after him, by playing the harlot after Molech. (Leviticus 20:2-5)

Very tough talk, but it shows how serious God was about disobedience among the Israelites. His first two commandments expressly prohibited the worshipping of any other "god" and in this passage He warns against the practice of human sacrifice to such gods and the penalties for disobedience.

We must remember that God was introducing Himself to the Israelites as a God who owned them, whether they liked it or not, and He had to be firm in order to establish the proper relationship between Him and His people. There weren't any negotiated conditions or suggestions. God commanded His people how they would live, and that was that. The penalties were swift and severe.

In verse 2, the penalty for offering one's child to an idol was death by stoning, to be administered by members of the congregation. The participants of that stoning were not doing wrong since God stated in verse 3 that He also would set His face against that man. This is one of the instances of a God-directed death penalty which He did not view as cruel and unusual punishment.

In verse 4 God stated that if the people remained indifferent toward such a crime and did not carry out the death penalty, then He would be against that man by cutting him off Himself (carrying out the death penalty) and all those who were in agreement with him.

Well, just imagine the national outcry against any who would suggest such a penalty for abortion. Look at what happens when some zealot bombs an abortion clinic or murders an abortion doctor. He is arrested, tried, and sentenced for murder, or the intention thereof, with his actions being condemned as a hate crime.

This is because our country is not a theocracy ruled by God, but a democracy with ever-changing laws to suit our current whims. Any violent actions based on scripture is widely condemned, and because of the status quo, I would certainly not advocate anyone taking the law into their own hands. In our system, the best response to abortion is to educate people on the moral wrongness of that issue and elect people to the judicial and legislative system that would be more sensitive to, and compliant with, God's word, rather than permitting and encouraging such immoral activity.

But until that could happen, we still have the problem of our nation sacrificing more than a million babies a year in violation of God's word and the general population doing nothing about it. Will God take matters into His own hands? And how would He do it?

Abortion has to do with children, and we have problems today with our children that where unheard of before the Supreme Court allowed the sacrifice of children in the womb to the idols of feminism and self-gratification.

Single parent homes, the manner of school education, drugs, a degrading culture, a lack of respect for human life, and a major lack of instruction in God's morality have been causing psychological problems in children that we aren't able to deal with, or, in many cases, do not even suspect. How can we expect all children to be normal and well-adjusted when so many of their brothers and sisters were given the death sentence while still in the womb? Could that be why they so easily kill each other and commit despicable acts against innocent people? Is that why they are no longer safe in school?

Who knows how God is working in the lives of people directly involved in the practice of abortion. Our worry should be that since it is a wide-spread, nationally accepted practice, perhaps God's response will involve the whole nation. If so, will it be a severe chastisement that brings us to repentance, or, if God knows (as He knows all things) that there will be no repentance, will we experience the full wrath of God in complete destruction?

Are we already in the beginning of such a response as evidenced by the terrorist attacks on our soil and against us around the world? Might the problems of energy, environmentalism, education, and economy result in the extinction of America as the light of the world, or at the least, reduce us to the status of a second- or third-rate nation?

God didn't allow the sins of Israel, His chosen people, the apple of His eye, to go unpunished. He brought one disaster after another upon them and banished them to a foreign land for 70 years. And finally, after enduring the final insult of rejecting the One whom He sent, Jesus the Christ, He dispersed them among the nations for 2,000 years.

We are a nation that was established and sustained by God. We have done more to evangelize the world than any other country, including Israel. We may have been the apple of His eye for two centuries, but after forsaking His word and committing the same types of sins as Israel, can we expect any better treatment? Not likely.

EPILOGUE

The ungodly liberal agenda has reached into every aspect of our lives. The powers that be, through unseen Satanic influence, are attempting to get control of everything we do. The liberal activists manipulate legislators, judges, educators, the news media, and the general public in much the same way as they are unknowingly manipulated themselves by Satan. So, what can we do about that?

For our struggle is not against flesh and blood, but against the rulers, against the powers, against the world forces of this darkness, against the spiritual forces of wickedness in the heavenly places. (Ephesians 6:12)

"Our struggle" is the war that is going on between God and Satan. What makes it so difficult for us is we can't see either of those beings or their subjects (angels and demons), nor can we see the realm where those forces operate. We can't take up arms to aid in any type of physical combat.

What we can do is heed the instruction given by God throughout His word, the Bible, on how to recognize and resist such activity in our earthly realm. In the earlier chapters of this book we have seen that there is a wealth of biblical information pertaining to the events of this world and the actions of men, particularly ungodly men. We can use that information to recognize their efforts of deception and make sure we don't enable them to continue in their deceit. That enabling factor is carried out during political elections.

The process is much like our bodies' circulatory system when the white blood cells turn cancerous and begin devouring the red cells to control the system. If it goes unchecked, the white cells will be victorious but the body will die. Christian men and women need to reject the cancerous liberal agenda at the ballot box, but as the liberals are voted out, God needs to be voted in, and that won't happen unless there is a national repentance, beginning in individual hearts.

Jesus said much to the people of Israel about how they lived, what rules and laws they lived by, and how they should treat one another, but He also told them that unless there was a change within their hearts there would not likely be any outward change. Most importantly, He strongly emphasized that the change was necessary for eternal life. His instruction on daily life was secondary to the matter of the kingdom of God.

Jesus told Nicodemus in John 3:3, *"Truly, truly, I say to you, unless one is born again, he cannot see the kingdom of God."*

To be born again is to be born of the Spirit. That transforming experience occurs only after one believes the word of God and accepts Jesus as the one who was sent to take away the sin of the world. It is a humbling experience, turning one's life over completely to God, but it is the only way. *"Truly I say to you, unless you are converted and become like children, you shall not enter the kingdom of heaven."* (Matthew 18:3)

It's hard for many folks to divest themselves of their adult independence and become like children, but that is the simple approach that God requires. Blind faith and child-like trust opens our minds to a spiritual world that does not exist in the mind of the unbeliever. Christians are seen as fools, needing the crutch of religion. *For the word of the cross is to those who are perishing foolishness, but to us who are being saved it is the power of God.* (I Corinthians 1:18)

There is nothing other than belief that changes us within and makes us fit for the kingdom of God. It is the only way to be saved, or "born again." There are no good works necessary for salvation and no other religion or savior that can deliver us. *And there is salvation in no one else; for there is no other name under heaven that has been given among men, by which we must be saved."* (Acts 4:12)

And that name is Jesus.

Salvation through Christ is not just an American thing. It is available to every man, woman, and child throughout the world.

But in every nation the man who fears Him and does what is right, is welcome to Him. (Acts 10:35)

"Turn to Me, and be saved, all the ends of the earth; For I am God, and there is no other." (Isaiah 45:22)

The basis for this book is God's response to the actions of the people of Old Testament Israel. They were His chosen people but God did not allow them to escape the penalties for sin and disobedience. The United States of America, with its great emphasis on the Christian religion, has been a "chosen" nation in God's sight. Will we not have to answer for committing the same wrongs as the Israelites?

The apostle Paul was not speaking to ancient Israel when he said, *"How shall we escape if we neglect so great a salvation? After it was at the first spoken through the Lord, it was confirmed to us by those who heard.* (Hebrews 2:3) Paul was speaking to people on this side of the cross which includes us today.

King David advised his son on the seriousness of the matter when he told him, *"As for you, my son Solomon, know the God of your father, and serve Him with a whole heart and a willing mind; for the Lord searches all hearts, and understands every intent of the thoughts. If you seek Him, He will let you find Him; but if you forsake Him, He will reject you forever.* (I Chronicles 28:9)

We can debate the atheist, feminist, homosexual, environmentalist, and any other liberal activist and vote such people out of office, but in the end, it all comes down to individual godly living. Beware of the sweet taste of liberal promises and entitlements. The bitterness of the outcome reveals the ungodly nature of the system.

The conclusion, when all has been heard, is: fear God and keep His commandments, because this applies to every person. (Ecclesiastes 12:13)